Affected
A Vagabond's Journey Through Life

People who and events which have had an impact on my life

PINNACLE-SYATT presents...

Affected
A Vagabond's Journey Through Life

People who and events which have had an impact on my life

written by
Ed Anderson

PINNACLE-SYATT Publications
San Marcos, CA

This book is dedicated to:

Nancy Glenning, an extraordinary friend who stepped forward to take care of me during the ninth inning of my life in my battle with cancer. It was her dedication and love, along with my PMA (Positive Mental Attitude), that has kept me going through these difficult times.

to:

The United States Marine Corps, which brought me out of my introverted shell, developed my character, provided the most excitement in my life, taught me about esprit de corps and camaraderie, and instilled the pride, tenacity, and "true grit" in me to weather the ordeals of the civilian world.

to:

My former ex-wives, official and unofficial,
Pat, for her dutiful tolerance, family building, and assisting my entry into adulthood.
Candy, for her timely beauty, Lamaze introduction and the raising of **Misty** in an exemplary manner, and subsequent personal growth to present day maturity.
Dona, for her vitality, early editorial inspiration, being my best friend for nine good years together, and for just "being there."
K.C., for her wisdom and knowledge, sensuality and class, and overall help in moving me forward.

to:

My parents, **Willis Drummond Anderson and Florence Lipinski Anderson**, both of whom are now deceased, who are not specifically mentioned in this book as people who affected me, but who jointly did the best they knew how to raise me to become a responsible, athletically oriented, and studious youngster. Parents sometimes screw up, as I have with my kids, but in retrospect their efforts were monumental and appreciated.

and finally to:

All three of my children, **Jeff, Michelle, and Misty**, the reasons I continue my struggle with this debilitating disease. I don't want to leave them quite yet. They each have taken different paths toward adulthood, have been the source of boundless and unconditional love for me, and each in their own way have made my life worthwhile. No father has more love for his kids than I do for each of them equally.

Foreword

The word is "affected," not "effected" (the difference between the two confuses many people, including me sometimes) or "infected," (this is not a book about disease or how to overcome its physical problems, although I am doing battle with a cancer as I write these words). Now that the title is squared away, I can explain why I am writing this book, article, or whatever it turns out to be.

Most people are affected by other people and/or events in their lives (let's just stick with the acceptable masculine version henceforth; otherwise it does get a bit cumbersome). The same is true for me. A while back (in September of 1995 to be precise), I was watching the tube, and there was Barbara Walters interviewing the actor Christopher Reeve in what was his first public appearance since his tragic and paralyzing accident. Like a lightning bolt, it struck me how inspiring Mr. Reeve's attitude was. Here's "Superman," a guy who had everything (on the surface. at least, to us vicarious admirers of the "rich and famous"), and who like that (snap your fingers for full effect) apparently had lost it all. Or had he? My first chapter is devoted to my thoughts about that interview, so I'll defer comment for a bit. Suffice to say, I was affected by his revelations and I thought I would put my thoughts to pen and paper. Especially given that it might provide readers, even if they are only family and the subjects of each chapter, some insight as to my inner thoughts as I approach the end of my trail.

That almost instantaneous inspiration for me obliged me to grab a pen and pad, jot down a few notes, and begin the thought process for perhaps writing an inspirational (I wasn't sure I could "inspire" readers-and I'm not now as I'm writing the words today) or revealing book of interest on how certain people and events have affected my life. I'm certainly not famous. I'm not an accomplished writer (although I've had a number of vocation oriented articles published in the past). I'm not sure if my experiences will be of an analogous value to anyone. And I don't know if this thing will ever get published. But I enjoy writing, so what the "hey." I'll give it a shot. My life has been diverse and interesting; maybe someone can benefit from reading about it.

I have no particular writing style, so I'm just going to wing it. The following chapters are in no particular order of importance, instead being chronological, for the most part. I hope the reader will find some value in these stories. If he is the type of reader who pays money for this type of publication, he should be looking for some sort of inspiration. That's why I go to a bookstore-to learn about a particular subject.

Table of Contents

Foreword

Preface

Chapter 1:   **Christopher Reeve**   *10*
His post-accident attitude caused me to write this book.

Chapter 2:   **Don Drysdale**   *12*
His death at 56 - my then age - awakened my recognition of one's
mortality.

Chapter 3:   **Howard Lynch**   *13*
My high school basketball coach, who developed my athletic skills and
toughened me up.

Chapter 4:   **Marianne: Teenage Years**   *16*
The rise and fall of first love.

Chapter 5:   **Moe Drabowski**   *20*
A major league awakening.

Chapter 6:   **Flight School Mid-Air**   *24*
The impact of watching death, and how it could have been me who
"brought the farm."

Chapter 7:   **Patricia Grant**   *26*
My mistreatment of wife number one and its later ramifications.

Chapter 8:   **Dick Chapman**   *28*
A Marine's Marine; a friend; an inspiration.

Chapter 9:   **November 22, 1963**   *30*
The impact of JFK's assassination on a young Marine.

Chapter 10:   **The Adoption Of My Son Jeff**   *32*
A 180 degree turn for me upon his arrival.

Chapter 11: **My Daughter Michelle's Maturation**   *34*
A progression from insecurity and drugs to a squared away attitude and
her impressive wedding.

Chapter 12: **June 30, 1970**   *38*
Discharge from the Marine Corps - the loss of esprit de corps and
camaraderie.

Chapter 13: **Suzanne and the FBI**   *43*
A Bureau vixen who finalized my marriage and re-introduced me to
love (infatuation?).

Chapter 14: **Arlene Wyatt: My Guru**   *45*
My initial exploration into self-improvement, self realization, and self-
actualization.

Chapter 15: **The Gallery and Wayne Bradshaw**   *47*
Bachelorhood on the beach.

Chapter 16: **Adjusting To Civilian Leadership (or lack thereof)**   *52*
An epic in frustration.

Chapter 17: **Christine: My Drinking Buddy**   *57*
Males and females can be friends.

Chapter 18: **Dudley and Covelle Jude**   *60*
One of my first civilian friends and her marriage to a draft-dodger.

Chapter 19: **Sue Dickinson: My Roomie**   *64*
The party giver who became a friend, roommate, and confidant
par excellence.

Chapter 20: **The Birth Of My Daughter Misty Dawn**   *69*
Ecstasy through Lamaze, with kudos to Candy, wife number two.

Chapter 21: **Dona: The Love Of My Life**   *75*
Paradise lost.

Chapter 22: **Frank Bell's Suicide**   *82*
The loss of my best friend.

Chapter 23: **Jim and Shirley Royer**   *85*
             The exceptions to a need for military commonality for friendship.

Chapter 24: **My Video Collection**   *89*
             A pacifying hobby or an expensive addiction? Both!

Chapter 25: **K.C. Anderson**   *93*
             A comprehensive excursion into "being in touch with my feelings" via
             wife number three.

Chapter 26: **Nancy Glenning**   *96*
             A God-send during my current illness; the impact of her love and
             friendship.

Author's Biography   *100*

Order Forms   *101*

Preface

I began this book in June 1996 (finishing it one month later), a short time after I began my chemotherapy treatment for the cancerous tumor at the base of my tongue. With this book, I've documented how certain people and events had an effect - usually positive - on my life. There were many more people and events which could have been inserted herein, but I chose these chapters as being the most significant. My life has been diverse and interesting; I could (and maybe will, if God grants me time) write separate books on some other people and events.

At present, I guess I am officially retired at age fifty-nine, given that the Social Security Administration has granted me permanent disability compensation, in view of my inability to verbally communicate in my latest vocational endeavors. The re-emergence of my tumor and the presence of massive scar tissue in my throat from the radiation treatment I underwent last year has restricted my speaking ability. For the past six years, I have been in outplacement services, writing resumes/letters and teaching clients how to effectively network, interview, and negotiate during their transition to a new job or career. It has been a calling I thoroughly enjoyed, especially given my writing skills/propensity. In fact, when I essentially went on a "medical leave of absence" from my last employer because of my illness and loss of strength/stamina/energy, I briefly opened my own business in that field, calling it "The Competitive Edge Company." My thrust had a bit of a twist, however. In order to substantially save my clients on the fee charged, I eliminated the database information concerning leads to business and people therein. That facet of the job search is a major selling point for larger outplacement service firms, but I knew that a client could get the information free-of-charge elsewhere, thereby saving himself a bundle of dollars. So I was optimistic about the viability of my new venture. Unfortunately, my speaking ability rapidly deteriorated due to the scar tissue aggravation. I had to put my business on hold. If all works out well for me in my battle with the cancer and I regain my voice and strength, perhaps I'll re-institute my business venture.

The above really doesn't have much to do with the essence of this book, but at least it brings the reader up to date regarding my status.

I finally want to say that my life has had its moments, both positive and negative. Despite the heartbreaks, disappointments, and recent disillusionment with my present medical status, I probably wouldn't change places with too many people, if any. It's been fun, sports fans! I want to acknowledge those people who comprise the bulk of these pages as the major players in my journey through life, and I want to reiterate my thanks for their presence, regardless of the outcome of each relationship. I am generally at peace with myself. I hope they all will think highly of me in their respective analyses of their lives.

Semper Fi.

Chapter 1   Christopher Reeve

He is the true inspiration for my taking pen in hand. I have been inspired by others in my past, for a variety of reason, but none of them have caused me to put my thoughts on paper (maybe it's a cumulative affect).

For the past year and a half, I have been doing battle with a cancer (tumor at the base of my tongue). I certainly have had my share of concerns, and I'm not out of the woods yet. An important aspect of my battle is maintaining a PMA (Positive Mental Attitude). It is a vitally essential ingredient in the "m.o." of anyone who is struggling to retain life. Without PMA, one is virtually giving up. I was fortunate in having learned about PMA a few years back. So I accepted the diagnoses and I entered the treatments in a very upbeat mode, which has generally been my attitude in my later years, even though some people who knew me in earlier days would disagree with that assessment.

To date, I have completed an extensive radiation treatment (my tumor was at the advanced stage when first detected and rather unique; meaning the initially stated odds for survival weren't that great in my favor), I have experienced the disappearance and then the reappearance of the tumor, and I am currently undergoing chemotherapy in an effort to buy some quality time. It ain't been pretty, but I'm optimistic that I'll see my three kids (Chapters 9, 10, and 20), who are all grown now, do something with their lives.

What does Christopher Reeve have to do with my health problems? Everything! I've briefly mentioned PMA and what it can do for someone with a problem ("challenge" is the right word to use, that is if you choose to be of a positive nature). His words, or more succinctly his attitude, was remarkable during the Barbara Walters interview.

Here's a guy who has been successful in his chosen field, has recently been married and become a father for the first and only time (to date - he says), has been idolized for his physical stature (I can't imagine too many other actors giving such credence to his Superman role), and has now been relegated to an electric wheelchair and life-sustaining respirators. What would your attitude be if you woke up to find yourself in his condition? I understand he went through the classic denial, anger, and remorse stages, but what's important is what I heard him say to Ms. Walters. Talk about PMA!

During my times of despair (even before the acquisition of the cancer), I've always thought back on a tour I once took at t he Los Angeles Children's Hospital. If you think you have it bad, go take a tour through a similar facility. If you have any empathy at all for children, it will tear your heart out. So part of my PMA is: If you think you have it bad, think about the kids in a Children's Hospital.

I guess I expected Christopher Reeve to utter words of despair, "Why me?" self-pity, and/or "my life sucks." Not Mr. Reeve. I don't know him or what his personality has been prior to the accident. They (whoever "they" are) say he is a nice guy, but one never knows about the

9

Who has the most late-1970s hair: the author
or "man's best friend," Sunshine?

Hollywood hype. His words, however, appeared to be spoken with sincerity. What words? I didn't write them down, but in essence he paraphrased Lou Gehrig's "I'm the luckiest man on this earth" in describing his approach to his situation. I was awe-struck. He's repeated that theme in several other interviews, so I imagine most Americans (and probably non-Americans) have heard or read about his positiveness. His philosophical perspective and his confidence about recovery are indeed to be admired, at the very least. For me, it was the ultimate in projecting a sense of what one of my favorite authors (Og Mandino) advocates as his five principles by which to live. To paraphrase Mr. Mandino, those principles are:

* Count Your Blessings
* Proclaim Your Rarity
* Use Your Freedom Of Choice Wisely
* Go That Extra Mile
* Do Everything With Love

Christopher Reeve should be an inspiration to us all. He is to me, and I am fully confident that his attitude will have him again walking, fathering children, and performing his endeavors of choice.

Chapter 2   Don Drysdale

Who - or what - should be the subject of Chapter 2? The first chapter sets the theme; the second should follow suit to the extent of being a logical (sometimes my logical being -left brain - has gotten in the way of my right brain passion, compassion, and creativity) and interest-bearing attention-getter. So I chose Don Drysdale, the former pitcher for the Dodgers and, until his demise, a recognized sports-caster. Not so much the individual, but the event of his death in 1993 is what struck me (no pun intended in view of his pitching skills).

This will be a short chapter because I don't want to dwell on a negative. Nevertheless, his death marked my recognition of my mortality. All of a sudden, here was this young (age is relevant, as it was for me in this case) man at age fifty-six - my then age - dying without giving anyone a clue that it was his time to go. No history of severe medical problems; a hearty and healthy appearing horse of a man.

Drysdale's passing made me realize that I wasn't a young whippersnapper anymore. Being a former athlete (I went to college on a basketball scholarship) and U.S. Marine Corps Officer and pilot, I have always prided myself in staying in pretty good shape (relatively speaking again) through proper exercise. I knew at age fifty-six I couldn't do the things I did in my teens and twenties (or even thirties and forties). I'm a realist. I usually pushed myself into an exercise regimen that had me feeling and looking pretty good at 6'4" and two hundred and five pounds, with low blood pressure, no smoking habit (but I do admit to having had a few rum-and-cokes as a social animal during my military and civilian days), and general good health.

But you never know when the grim reaper is going to get you. You certainly can't worry about it, as that will enhance your chances for medical problems (the mind controls the body). I have always had the philosophical perspective of "If your time is up, it's up; there's nothing you can do about it, so don't worry about it." Live life to the fullest is the motto I've advocated. Your turn will eventually come, but not to worry in the meantime. I was - and am - a believer that if you exercise and watch what you were eating, your body will take care of itself. The ironic counter-thought to that is, I have known young (a twenty-eight-year-old physical fitness buff of a Marine) and relatively young (a mid-forties USMC general) men whose untimely deaths during an exercise program, have illustrated that a finely-tuned body is not the only measure for physical fitness.

But, you know, it was Don Drysdale's death which marked my recognition that I wasn't getting any younger and you never know when your time is up. The significant aftermath of his passing for me was that it precipitated my taking pen in hand and writing my "final" words to each of my children individually (to be given to them at the time of my death). I wanted each to have those last words, even if I lived for another hundred years and the words were no longer relevant. It's the thought that counts!

This chapter and this even is not inspirational, but it did affect me to the extent of mortality recognition. That morbid fact hits each of us at different times. My point is that it should serve us all to take stock of our lives.

Chapter 3   Howard Lynch

Beginning with this chapter, I think I'll revert to the chronological presentation of significant people and events in my life, rather than order of importance. If I chose that latter method, some people might get their noses bent out of shape. Also, the reader may not wish to read the last couple of chapters, believing them to be of lesser importance, no matter how adroitly (hopefully) I wrote the material.

For my next person, I go back to that wonderful institution called high school. I don't mean to imply sarcasm here, as I - unlike others - do regard high school as a positive time. Growing; yes. Learning; yes. Being an athletic hero; yes. Being embarrassed; yes. (I was not the same person then as I am now). Having fun, without much responsibility; yes (although I do modify that, because the responsibility of being a high school athletic "star" had its impact). Being sophisticated in boy-girl relationships or general dating and awareness of "carnal knowledge;" not only no, but hell no (although I was "going steady" with one young lady - the subject of my next chapter - for most of my high school days).

There were many people who influenced me during my adolescent period as a teenager. Certainly my parents in a variety of ways, but I choose not to identify them as people who "affected" me, because all parents affect their children. I also had some interesting teachers in high school, and I could probably write a book on my peers. But the one person who was most instrumental in "affecting" me was my basketball coach. Howard Lynch by name, a business administration teacher by trade, and a basketball coach almost by default.

Many people sing the praises of John Wooden at UCLA. Rightfully so, both as a coach and as a teacher - not of academia, but of human values and methods of attaining success. Everyone should study Mr. Wooden's "Pyramid of Success." Howard Lynch did not get this notoriety at the college level, but he certainly deserved similar accolades at the high school level. I cannot think of anyone else whom I would praise for his insights about people (especially teenagers), his skill in coaching (especially since I don't believe he was trained as a coach), and his motivational acumen for leading a wide range of characters toward championship caliber basketball.

Why was he so special? Let me give you a couple of illustrations that come immediately to mind.

In those days (in early fifties New York), freshmen usually didn't play varsity ball in any sport, regardless of their proficiency. That was fine with me because I really didn't take up the game of basketball until I was twelve or thirteen (most kids start much younger), so I wasn't that great, even at a small school. My father - although he played basketball as a youth (In fact, he played with the legendary Joe Lapchick, for those of you who really know your basketball history.) - was more of a baseball fanatic. So that's what he taught me from almost day one. I can still remember tossing the baseball around with him, as well as his general instruction about coordination and body movement.

I had participated in some sort of intramural or summer basketball as a twelve-thirteen year old,

14

learning the fundamental techniques from a man by the name of Cliff Balcolm, who was the coach for the local Recreation Commission. So I was prepared for high school basketball in regards to knowing the rules, the basic fundamentals, and the dedication to the sport. It was Howard Lynch, however, who took me to that next level.

I was a rather shy and non-aggressive person as a teenager. Socially I didn't improve much from age thirteen until the time I entered college. Mr. Lynch recognized that as a skinny 6'2", one hundred and forty pound freshman who was basically afraid of the tougher kids, I was not exactly the classic power forward, rebound getter, or "hatched man" that we all recognize among today's NBA (National Basketball Association, for you non-jock straps) elite. What initially impressed me - now in retrospective reflection and during my real-time adventure on the court as a thirteen year old - was Mr. Lynch's knowledge of the fundamentals. I was not a product of inner-city razzle-dazzle, nor was I even a product of undisciplined "summer leagues" that are so prevalent today. One of the basic problems with many of our basketball heroes today is their lack of the knowledge of fundamentals. I watch today's rebounding game, for instance, and am amazed that most players don't have the foggiest idea about "boxing out."

Mr. Lynch stressed fundamentals. He taught them verbally and through constant drills. Where he learned these rudimentary necessities for success, I really don't know. I never thought to ask in those days as a teenager; I just followed the leader. Perhaps it was his methodology for teaching those disciplined fundamentals which provided me with the tools for basketball success, as well as for an appreciation for discipline and knowing the fundamentals in life's other ventures in my future.

I remember one "drill" which was instrumental in my moving forward in basketball skills. As I mentioned, I was a rather shy and non-aggressive youngster. That doesn't hack it on the basketball court. Mr. Lynch would watch me grab a rebound, only to lose it to a more aggressive player who would simply wrestle the ball from me. He knew I needed to be toughened up. So what he did was have (by virtue of a meeting with my teammates unbeknownst to me) all nine of the other players on the practice court intentionally bang my body, not only for a rebound, but at anytime. I finally figured out that the style of play I was witnessing was not the norm. It only took a goodly number of bumps and bruises for me to learn how to protect the ball, and actually how to go get the ball off the board - and hold on to it - in a fashion that I had not perceived before. Mr. Lynch's clandestine drill did wonders for initiating this timid kid into the real world (both in basketball and life) or assertiveness. It didn't change my personality (I was still the "victim" of a domineering mother), but it certainly sharpened my skills on the court. I doubt that I would have gained a collegiate basketball scholarship otherwise. I had the grace and finesse to be a fundamentally good ballplayer, but without a tenacity to make myself physically known on the court, I would have been simply pushed into obscurity and oblivion.

So thanks, Mr. Lynch, wherever you are. I wish I had kept in contact with you through the years. I imagine he's gone on to coach on heavenly courts by now; I just hope that he had that innate knowledge that he was appreciated.

Mt. Kisco High School coach, Howard Lynch (right rear standing)
with nucleus of 1952-1953 NY Tri-County Championship Team
(author is second from left, middle row seated)

Chapter 4   Marianne: Teenage Years

Ah, first love! Actually, I had a couple of excursions into "puppy love" with, as I recall, two other twelve to fourteen year old young ladies in junior and early-senior high school. Not that I learned anything about relationships or physicalness - man, was I naive! I don't even recall how Marianne and I became "involved." (Note: As a matter of discretion, I am deleting her surname.) It must have been a result of my developing into a local basketball and baseball hero, and she being the peppy cheerleader. It's not really important how we met. What's important is that Marianne and I learned together about high school love/romance, the wonderfulness of companionship and reliance upon each other, and the inevitable (I suppose, given the circumstances) heartbreak of separation.

What Marianne saw in me, I'll never know. She was really the most popular girl in school, being physically attractive, with a vivacious and effervescent personality that drew everyone to her. Granted, we lived in a small town and our entire high school population was around two hundred. But I venture to say she would have been equally popular in a larger setting. She just had that magnetism that people admired and sought out.

I should not demean myself, however. I suppose I could have been described as attractive as well, in a boyish way. Tall, baby-faced, a successful student, sincere, and one of the star athletes of the school. I certainly was not a sophisticated kid, even by fifties standards. I knew nothing of the joys of sex, as my folks never discussed the subject and there was no such a thing as sex education in the school system in those days.

Marianne, despite her popularity and more "street-wise" awareness, was also not aware of sexual things. At least not with me, and I'm confident not with anyone else (we had one major "break-up" and a couple of minor spats during our three years as a couple which led her to dating others). Our mutual physical attraction - and it was as passionate as we could get, based on our limited knowledge, and truly a product of love as we knew it - entailed heavy "petting" only. In other words, we knew each other's body without actual intercourse or the application of love-making techniques that we all eventually learn later in our progression in that arena. And we sought out time for our excursions into that new-found joy. We even had our own favorite place out in the boondocks for "parking." I imagine we were the envy of other couples in that mode, given that hat my folks had a Nash Rambler, the first vehicle which had reclining front seats. Instant bed! Too bad it wasn't utilized to the maximum.

I suppose I could write volumes about Marianne and our activities, despite my poor memory. She, or should I say my "first love," affected me in numerous ways. As Shakespeare wrote: "How do I love thee? Let me count the ways." Marianne did that for me, and probably had as great an influence on me as any woman ever had in my future. She taught me - or better yet, we learned together - about love (in all its wondrous ways, regardless of our limited experience at the time), about the tenderness associated with loving someone (although it was many, many years later and after a couple of failed marriages before I really became educated in interpersonal relationships, as well as in "Men Are From Mars; Women Are From Venus" precepts), about the ecstasy of what it means to be "going steady" (e.g., mutual confidence in your mate; being there for your best friend/mate in good and bad times), about communicating without boundaries (which is actually the basis for any relationship, which, sad to say, comes on deaf ears in fifty percent of marriages/relationships in today's environment), about holding hands in public (one of the small things necessary in a demonstrative relationship), about walking (her home was $1\frac{1}{2}$ miles from school) together arm-in-arm while discussing who knows what, about planning for the future without really knowing what it takes to do so, and finally about heartache (ranging from momentary fights about misunderstandings, to misperceived allegiances, to the eventual demise of a relationship).

I'll conclude this chapter by relating the circumstances of our final farewell and how that affected me in my growth pattern. I was a year ahead of Marianne in school. I went to "prep-school" in Massachusetts for a year (to hone my basketball skills before exploring college scholarships) following my graduation from high school. We saw each other a few times during that year, and we did correspond to a limited extent. Unfortunately, the misperceived allegiances which I mentioned above had me align with a new school friend and fellow basketball junkie instead of Marianne during a school break. That normally would finalize a relationship, but upon our respective graduations we found each other again, briefly. Soon thereafter, Marianne advised me that she was leaving New York (I had committed to Trinity College in Hartford, CT) with her mother, who had a bad case of asthma, to seek out a warmer, dryer climate in the west. What a shock! I figured we would have four years of my attending college to have a continuing relationship and plan for the future together. But I guess at age seventeen, she had to acquiesce to her mother's wishes.

Our final night together still stands out vividly in my mind. It was my initiation to true heartbreak. It wouldn't be my last, but it was probably the most significant and revealing as the first. We were sitting in my folks' Rambler outside her home trying to say good-bye (they were leaving for California the next day). I have never cried so much in my entire life. This was the most important person in my life, and she was leaving forever (we were too naive to recognize that letters, phone calls, and perhaps visits during my college years might save the relationship). I don't remember what we talked about; I'm sure we covered a myriad of topics. What stands in the forefront - even to this day - is the agony we both went through in saying good-bye. If such heartbreak was so devastating at age seventeen-eighteen (respectively), what trauma would we each experience in the future? It was indeed dramatic and mind-boggling, to say nothing of that feeling of being "lost." As a footnote, I've had a few similar farewells as an adult, but I believe I was more prepared for them with a few of life's experiences under my belt by then. Nothing could compare to saying good-bye forever to Marianne; nothing affected me so passionately (in a negative fashion) as that single night.

But life moves on. I actually saw Marianne once about six or seven years later. We never kept in touch during my college years (how dumb of me!), but I learned that she, her sister Rachel, and her mother (her father, who was lacking in loyalty, stayed behind in New York to pursue his own life) had settled in Tucson, AZ. By then (1961 or '62) I was a young Marine Corps Officer and pilot.

Author (#12) demonstrating skills in high school basketball.
Photo by Marianne

I wrote to her and arranged a meeting in Tucson. I flew there in my helicopter from my base in Santa Ana, CA (now Marine Corps Air Station - Tustin, a sub-station of MCAS El Toro). I was met at the Officers Club of Tucson's Davis-Monthan Air Force Base by Marianne's husband (she had informed me of her marriage during our reintroductory correspondence). Funny, it didn't bother me that she was now married (as I was) with children (two, as I recall). Perhaps I recognized the inevitability of it, given our lack of correspondence during my collegiate days. Her husband drove me to their home. Our reunion was cordial, but formal. Marianne and I did have an hour or so alone together to discuss our past and current lives. We could both see that the special spark was gone. We also both shed a couple of tears for what could have been. C'est la vie! I never saw or heard from Marianne again, although I tried a couple of times through the years. As recently as 1992 I was informed by her sister that Marianne, who was now a grandmother, no longer thought about her past. How sad; or maybe I'm just too sentimental about the past (tears are flowing as I write this). How different our lives might have been if we had just made the effort to stay in touch following her departure that heartfelt day in 1955.

Ed and Marianne
Senior Prom 1954

Chapter 5   Moe Drabowski

I thought I was a real hot-shot of a ball player. I've already documented in Chapter 3 my young learning curve from my dad's instruction, through the home-town Recreation Commission and high school heroics, to my acceptance of a basketball scholarship to college. Basketball became my number one choice, but baseball was genetically ingrained in me because of my father's preference. I related in that and the subsequent chapter how I was a high school star in both sports. It was my intention to not only honor my scholarship obligation in the larger round ball game, but to also apply my prowess in the national pastime while at Trinity College. I was, after all, a pretty good first-baseman and a proven hitter at that lower scholastic level.

I suppose my initial glorification (self-imposed, to be sure, with a little help from my folks) in Abner Doubleday's brain-child occurred at age fifteen. (Note: in retrospect, I think it ironic that my college senior history thesis - I was a history major in my liberal arts education, following my freshman year try at math - focused on Doubleday's career as an Army officer and concurrent inventiveness into this thing he called "baseball," given my later abbreviated military career and the revelation in the paragraphs below.) I had already established myself as a rising star on the basketball court and baseball diamond by the time I was a sophomore in high school. That summer of 1952, my ballooned evaluation of myself was enhanced during a "try-out" held in my hometown of Mt. Kisco, NY by the Chicago Cubs. Every teenager in the county who had any baseball skills whatsoever probably attended that training camp. I must have done well. At the conclusion of the drills, the head scout exhibited interest in my abilities (or potential). Probably believing me to be seventeen or eighteen, he asked me how old I was. Being a straight-forward and naive sort of chap, I responded with "I'm fifteen." Well, that put an end to that. Even in those days, high school baseball players were signed up by major league teams for their farm systems. But not normally at fifteen. The scout did, however, offer me encouragement by stating words to the effect: "Come see me in a couple of years." It bloated my ego and made me feel rather special. I didn't realize that he probably said the same thing to a million other kids in his scouting sessions throughout the country.

I took him seriously, however. Although my skills in and love for basketball were surpassing my lesser affinity for baseball, much to the chagrin of my father, I developed into a rather good hitter and first baseman. As I recall, I batted something like .455 in my senior year and scooped up many an errant throw from the other infielders. I didn't achieve the county/state wide recognition in baseball as I did in basketball, which should have told me something, but didn't. So after continued athletic success in prep school for the year following my graduation from Mt. Kisco High, I envisioned that I would be a two-sport hero in college.

Freshmen could not play varsity level ball in college (as well as in high school) in the '50s. Consequently, I was relegated to the freshman squad in both sports at Trinity. No problem; no earth shattering setbacks. That was the norm, so I accepted it as the routine in my growth pattern. Without elaboration, I'll simply say that I was successful in both sports during my freshman year - with one proviso. And a major one at that, both literally and figuratively.

It has been well documented by many professional athletes in their "life stories" that making the transition from one level to another (e.g., from high school to college; from college to the pros) can be a difficult one. My eyes became vividly widened to that truism. I adjusted well on the basketball court, although with better coaching I could have further improved my game. But baseball was another matter, primarily because of the presence of one man named Moe Drabowski.

Unless you are a real baseball history aficionado, you may not remember his name. Moe was a major league pitcher. He played for several teams, but gained particular notoriety in the mid-sixties when he was a reliever for the Baltimore Orioles (I'm quite sure that was the team for which he made his mark). His major accomplishment came in the World Series in which he set a Major League (maybe it was just the American League - I'm not too adept at stats) record for consecutive strikeouts by a reliever in a World Series game. His fantastic achievement. which I happened to watch on TV, was truly a remarkable feat. It certainly provided unexpected drama to the game and jubilation for Orioles fans. In fact, I remarked to myself and to my associates (whoever they were at that time) who watched the game with me that Moe was the reason that I stopped playing baseball in college.

Turning the reel backwards. I was introduced to Moe Drabowski on the Trinity College diamond. I was a self-described freshman hot-shot who could hit anybody. Moe was a senior who had already attracted numerous scouts the year before. He could throw the ball through a brick wall. A strong-armed right-hander, Moe not only had a lively fastball, but he also had a demented sense of humor regarding "brushing back" a hitter. Moe kept a hitter on his toes - and many times on his backside. You could say that Moe was a wild man, in personality and in pitching. He had a very congenial air about himself, and he loved life. His reputation in the Major League. as I understand it, was that of a prankster and reveler, who paid as much attention to the statistics of the female "groupies" as he did to the propensities of the opposing hitters.

Could this skinny Mt. Kisco High School senior hit Moe Drabowski two years later? For answer, see text.

22

Well, I learned the hard way that I wasn't the hot-shot I thought I was at the plate. I suppose I had faced mediocrity in high school and had a false sense of ability as I progressed to college (and possibly to the big leagues?). I could hit the other Trinity varsity pitchers, but I couldn't even see the "apple" when Moe delivered it. I imagine he was throwing in the upper ninety mile per hour range in college; I believe he exceeded that in the pros. That in itself is overwhelming. But add to it his penchant for being inconsistent in knowing where the plate was (intentionally or otherwise), standing sixty feet away from his whipping arm delivery was horrifying, even for someone like myself who thought he could deal with it. I think I hit Moe a couple of times during our intra-squad games, but standing there at the plate taught me a lesson in humility - or fear!

A funny thing happened on my way to the majors. I quit. In doing so, I knew I was letting my dad down. But reality prevailed. Perhaps with better coaching (same-same for collegiate basketball for me advancing to the NBA) I might have gone further. I just fell apart in my sophomore year, however. I had a lock on the 1st-base position, based on my success as a freshman. Something happened to me during the pre-schedule practices. Moe had graduated, so I didn't have to face him again, and we didn't have any other pitcher in his category. But all of a sudden, I grew very apprehensive about being "beaned" by an errant fastball. In fact, I didn't even like to handle a normal pick-off throw from the pitcher. I had lost my confidence. When that happens to any athlete in any sport, He has to either "hang it up" or work his way through his problem. I chose the lesser of the two evils, as I viewed it. It was a tough decision and I felt like I was letting my teammates down (let alone my dad, as I mentioned). But I had "lost it," and no amount of persuasion could convince me to "tough it out."

That was the end of my baseball career, mostly thanks to the reality of Moe Drabowski's super fastball. Moe was an exceptional college player, as proved by his success in the pros. Perhaps I should have learned to adjust and improve, based upon his affect on me. I always knew there was a "faster gun in the west," meaning better ball players than I out there. I accepted the fact that I could learn from better basketball players (and I did), but it didn't happen in baseball. I've experienced a heck of a lot more pain (e.g., sprained ankles) playing basketball that I ever did in baseball, so I guess the vision of taking one between the eyes petrified me enough to leave that game. I have been involved in numerous softball leagues in subsequent years, but it's not the same as facing a Moe Drabowski fastball with your name written on the stitches.

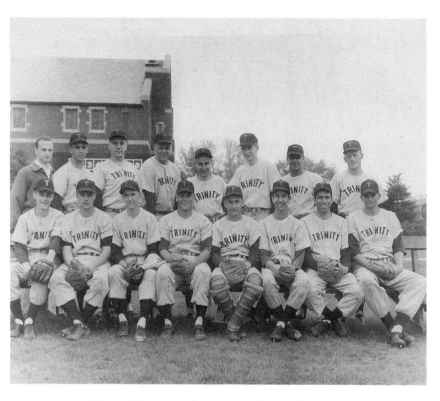

Trinity College Freshman Baseball Team —Spring, 1956
(Author is seated at the far right)

Chapter 6   Flight School Mid-air

I have many interesting stories I could tell about my attendance at the Marine Corps OCS (Officer Candidate School) and the Naval Flight School. Some are hilarious and others are harrowing (with a few, like the context of this chapter, horrifying). They in themselves could make excellent chapters for a separate book about my military experience. The purpose of this book, however, is to relate how an individual or event "affected" my life. I guess you could say that observing, and almost becoming a part of, a mid-air aircraft accident could have and affect on oneself.

Let me paint the scenario. I was in advanced flight training at Whiting Field, which is a part of the NAS (Naval Air Station) Pensacola complex in the panhandle portion of Florida (the southern red-neck attitude - at least in those days - was more Alabama than Florida, given that Pensacola was a scant few miles from Mobile). I had completed the ground school and basic training portions of the syllabus. At Whiting Field we were taught the rudiments of formation flying and airborne gunnery tactics. The aircraft we flew in advanced training was the T-28, a propeller-driven, piston engine horse of a platform. The capabilities of the aircraft made it almost equivalent to anything that the U.S. flew in World War II and the Korean conflict (except for the jets). I was about mid-way to completion of the formation syllabus when I experienced a most enlightening aspect of the innate dangers associated with flying. There exists an expression that paraphrases something like this: "Aviation is ninety-nine percent unadulterated boredom and one percent sheer terror." The routineness of flying can sometimes lull one into a false sense of comfort or complacency. If you ever reach that point - watch out! You can never let your guard down or be unprepared for the eventualities of something getting screwed up, which can lead to disaster and loss of life. "Be prepared" is a good motto for a Boy Scout, and it is a mandatory realism in aviation. Otherwise, to use some aviation/military vernacular, "your ass is grass," or "you've bought the farm," or several other expressions pertaining to the imminence of death.

I was a solo pilot part of a four aircraft section which had just completed its hour and a half excursion into the wild blue yonder practicing the various facets of formation flying. At the beginning of the flight, I was in the third aircraft. Toward the conclusion of an uneventful "hop," the number one aircraft experienced radio problems. Per procedures, he passed the lead to the number two pilot, number one now assuming the number four slot. I naturally moved up to the number two position, which was on the right wing of the new number one bird. As we were proceeding homeward, the new number one pilot started to also experience radio problems. As he was about to pass the lead to me, he regained radio communications. Little did I know it at the time, but his resumption of the lead saved my life, and unfortunately for him, cost him his life.

Whiting Field had crowded skies. It was a busy airfield. Normally the aircraft controllers in the tower are thoroughly vigilant in their duties. They have to be. Even though they are junior enlisted people (as opposed to Officers), usually with a more senior enlisted supervisor in charge, they have a tremendous amount of responsibility. But that's what training is all about. If one is properly trained, no matter what his job, the potential for negativism is minimized. Well, it didn't happen that day. Somebody in the tower screwed up.

As our section of four aircraft approached the airfield, our new leader, who could have been me if he had not regained use of his radio communications, called for clearance to enter the pattern. He received an affirmative and we proceeded across the field, individually broke off from the four plane formation, and entered the "dog leg" (parallel to the runway) in preparation for banking into the straight-away for touchdown on the runway.

As my leader was descending into the "dog leg," I (in my number two position) could see four other T-28s taking off from Whiting. I knew something was amiss, but before I could "sound off" on the radio, tragedy struck. Right before my eyes, the leader of the section of four taking off climbed directly into my descending leader. From his descending mode relative to the outbound aircraft, he couldn't see his counterpart approach his airspace. My eyes widened as I watched the climbing T-28 mesh his propeller into the tail section of my leader's fuselage. It was like watching a movie. Unreal! I couldn't believe it. With the loss of his tail section, my leader plummeted straight down into the ground from about one thousand feet. He didn't have a chance. Possibly he could have bailed out if he reacted quickly enough. There were no ejection seats in the T-28, like in a jet aircraft; you had to physically jettison the canopy and jump. But he didn't jump, and I watched him "buy the farm." I also observed the climbing aircraft, whose prop was now non-functioning for all intents and purposes, try to swing back to the runway for an emergency landing. He gave it a valiant try, but at the last few hundred feet, he too dove straight into the ground.

Fortunately for me, the training I had already received about reacting to an emergency (of any kind) sunk in. I didn't panic. I radioed my observations to the tower, received instructions to take the remainder of my section into a holding pattern away from the airfield, and awaited further instructions. Because of the extended duration of the flight now, we were all critically low on fuel. Fortunately, the tower had gotten itself organized, in conjunction with dispatching the crash crew and all other airborne aircraft, and advised us to return to base. By the time I touched down and taxied to the flight line, I was virtually out of gas (personally, as well as the aircraft).

I knew the two pilots who were killed. They weren't close personal friends, but when a comrade goes down, it affects us all. Interestingly, it could have been me who "bought the farm." If the new number one had not regained his radio, I would have been number one. I didn't ask him, as I recall, but I wonder if number four (who started off the flight as number one) similarly thought about the "fickle finger of fate" which spared us, but cost another his life.

Chapter 7   Patricia Grant

This chapter and the next are interrelated. Since my meeting of and marriage to Pat Grant came before I joined the Marine Corps and subsequently met Dick Chapman, I'll do this in a chronological manner.

It is not so much my marriage to Pat (my first) that had an affect on me. It was more of a present retrospective view of how I mistreated her that has had an impact on my current being that I wish to relate.

First wife, Pat.

I met Pat during the summer of 1959. I had graduated from college in June and was awaiting orders from the Marine Corps to report to OCS (Officer Candidate School). Not expecting those orders until the fall, I became a lifeguard at the local swimming pool to while away my time. Someone had told me about a very attractive young lady of a lifeguard at another pool in an adjacent town. I explored, I wooed, and I became engaged at Christmas, following my commissioning as a Second Lieutenant at OCS at the Marine Corps Base in Quantico, VA. We were married seven months later during my flight training at NAS Pensacola, FL.

I'm not devoting a lengthy chapter to Pat, even though I was "with" her longer than any relationship I've had (thirteen years). I think what I'm doing herein is offering an apology to Pat, indirectly, for the abuse I put her through. I've learned much about interpersonal relations, marriage, and communications since Pat and I divorced. I certainly was not the same person then as I am now. The effect that Pat and that relationship had on me is therefore one of a transitory nature. Without the presence of Pat and concurrently the Marine Corps, I suppose I may have never realized that a person can learn and grow, if he wants to.

When I say I "abused" Pat, I don't mean that I physically abused her (I only slapped her once, toward the end of our life together, and that was when she had become hysterical about learning of my "extra-curricular activities"). I'll have to admit that my behavior could be classified as mentally abusive, however. But I could also cop out by saying I was the victim of circumstances. I should have known better; I just didn't.

As stated, my life with Pat was concurrent to my life as a Marine Corps Officer and pilot. My first love (or devotion, if you will) was to the Marine Corps. I was indoctrinated! Most Marines are. It is difficult being a Marine's wife. First of all, there's the constant and lengthy separation. In those days, a Marine helicopter pilot could expect to be gone overseas for thirteen months every two to four years (my USMC tenure coincided with the Vietnam fiasco). That's not easy on the wife, especially if she is raising a family by herself during those times of overseas deployment. Secondly, my devotion to the Marine Corps and the Marine Corps way of doing things proved disastrous to the relationship.

I was not well versed (hell, I wasn't versed at all) in, as I've said, interpersonal relationships, the tenets of what makes a marriage work, and the communications necessities that help transcend the difficulties. On top of that, it was my way or no way. If we had friends, they were my Marine Corps friends (its not that she wasn't "allowed" to have friends outside of the Corps; I just didn't acknowledge them). I was a macho, chauvinistic pig when it came to the events of our life together. I never considered her or her preferences. I don't know how she put up with it all as long as she did without saying something (she was very demure in that sense). Being of a submissive personality was probably her basic fault, which was unusual for a well-educated registered nurse. And of course my "take-charge" gung-ho attitude didn't help her break out of her shell.

So it was the blind leading the blind. Even when I recognized that we were having trouble, I (actually we) didn't take the necessary steps (e.g., marriage counseling) with whole-hearted enthusiasm and sincerity to remedy the situation. It was inevitable that our marriage wouldn't last (it still amazes me that some military marriages do have longevity). And it didn't. There is no need to detail the circumstances of how the marriage concluded. That's not the point of this chapter. The affect that my first divorce had on me was that it finally precipitated an awakening in me that there was more to a relationship than what I had known or experienced. Meaning that my new-found vision caused me to seek out therapy, all by my lonesome. Which I did for the first few months of my bachelorhood. It was a priority for me, even taking precedence over my pursuing the joys of bachelorhood in Hermosa Beach, CA. Remember, I got married right out of college and didn't have an adult years bachelorhood. Pat stayed in Seattle, WA, the site of my first duty station with the FBI, following my abbreviated eleven year career in the Marine Corps.

So to Pat I say: "I'm truly sorry that I mistreated you." I also am thankful to her for several other things, as you will read about in subsequent chapters, as well as for introducing me to the enlightenment of self-improvement and personal therapy/counseling.

28

Chapter 8   Dick Chapman

The first time I saw Dick Chapman, I said to myself: "Now there is what a Marine is supposed to look like!" Little did I know that we would soon be squadron mates and he would become one of my closest friends, of all-time. I had seen a variety of Marines before that introduction. In fact, my recruiter in college was the primary reason I joined the Marine Corps following my college graduation.

That recruiter's name was (still is) Dick Cooke. At the time he was a Captain, a designated Naval Aviator (All Marine pilots are Naval Aviators, since we go through the same training at the same facilities as our Navy counterparts. The Marine Corps is operationally a part of the Navy,) and the recruiter out of New York City who had the responsibility to recruit potential officers (and potential pilots) from east coast universities/colleges. Captain Cooke was one squared-away Marine, as was his grunt associate, also a spunky (compared to Cooke's matter-of-fact demeanor) Italian Captain whose name escapes me for the moment.

I didn't know much about the military as a college student. Since I didn't have any definitive plans for a civilian career (What is one going to do with a liberal arts education, but no particular focus?), I talked with all of the recruiters from all of the services who visited the campus at Trinity College in Hartford, CT. Captain Cooke (he is now a retired Major General) took the time to explain the program and some of the exemplary tradition/history of the Marine Corps. Hearing stories about the the various battles in which Marines participated, and learning how the Air Wings of the Corps support their cohorts on the ground, was simply inspirational. For me, neither the Army, Air Force, nor the Navy could match those "sea stories." Furthermore, there was something about the Marine uniforms that turned me on (still does). So that was it. I signed the papers to enter AOC (Air Officer Candidate) program (Getting paid more than the grunts didn't hurt my decision making either, although I had never even been in an aircraft of and kind,) with a projected attendance at the OCS in the fall of fifty-nine.

In retrospect, I wouldn't have done anything different. To be a part of that organization, with its pride, esprit-de-corps, and camaraderie was the thrill of my life. As soon as I got a taste of the Marine Corps life, including the flying, I was committed. Still am. "Once a Marine, always a Marine." I just wish I had put in at least twenty years (for retirement benefits), but I only stayed for eleven, and that's another story.

As a side note, I ran into then Brigadier General Cooke in 1980 or 1981, when I joined the Marine Corps Aviation Association. General Cooke was the Commanding General of Marine Corps Air Station El Toro at the time. We saw each other at an MCAA function. Of course, I recognized him right away. Not knowing if he would remember me, I introduced myself and told him that he was my recruiter. He remembered (I guess his mental capacity is one reason why he was promoted to that august rank.) and we spent a few hours together at subsequent events. He was indeed an outstanding Marine. But more on a personal note was the impression Dick Chapman made on me. I had recently graduated from flight school, earned my "Wings of Gold," and had been assigned to the then (1961) Marine Corps Air Facility at Santa Ana. That base housed Marine Air Group 36, which was the helicopter arm of Marine Corps Air Station - El Toro, the site of the fixed wing fighter, attack, and transport aircraft.

My initial squadron was HMH-462, whose helicopters were a larger troop and cargo carrying bird. A couple of weeks after my arrival at Santa Ana, the Group held some kind of multi-squadron briefing (I believe it concerned the new Vietnam conflict and the Marine Corps response to it). As I peered over the large contingent of officers, Dick Chapman, who was attached to another squadron, walked past me. Maybe it was a premonition that this man would become a close personal friend, otherwise I'm not sure what struck me about Dick. His appearance (like General Cooke's a couple of years earlier) was exemplary: A crisp uniform, a gait that exuded confidence, and a warm smile for his "companos."

I had been stationed with a goodly number of other Marine officers during OCS and flight training. In fact, I already had made a few good friends, one being a gent by the name of Ken Babbs. The affinity that Ken and I had was our mutual love of the game of basketball. He played at Miami of Ohio, and we both played for the NAS Pensacola team during flight training. Ken was somewhat of a rebel also, which was an attraction for me (I've been known, especially as a civilian, as a "rabble-rouser" due to my non-conformity on matters which I considered needed change, but that didn't fully develop in me until years later.) Ken, however, "fought the program" from day one. He also indulged in some heavy-duty drugs (which I learned about later on) and upon discharge from the Marine Corps joined Ken Kesey's (the author of "One Flew Over The Cuckoo's Nest" and "Sometimes A Great Notion") crowd of merrymen on the infamous psychedelic "bus." If you're interested in learning more about that crowd, read Tom Wolfe's "The Electric Kool-Aid Acid Test" and Ken Babb's "The Bus."

Returning to Dick Chapman. Following that MAG-36 assembly where I first saw Dick, we were both re-assigned to HMM-163, a squadron of medium sized helicopters which was designated to become an "advisor" to the Vietnamese a year hence. During that intense training period of 1961-62, the officers of 163 became a pretty tight-knit group. There were individual sub-groups of course, as would happen in any organization of about fifty individuals (The squadron had about fifty officers and two hundred enlisted men.) I'm not sure how Dick and I became friends, but one of the sub-groups I mentioned included Dick and me. My admiration for Dick's professionalism, for his engaging personality that drew everyone to him, and for his liking of the "let's party" attitude, along with us playing basketball together on the squadron team, were the credentials that I sought for friendship. Fortunately for me, Dick responded in kind, not only during the three years of sharing experiences together in the squadron, both stateside and in Vietnam, but in our respective civilian lives as well. (He retired in Hawaii and I moved about.) As is typical in the military, we lost track of each other because of different assignments, but I still - to this day - regard Dick and his wife Charlene as two of my best friends. And more than that, I still am reminded (I look back on my USMC days as the best time of my life.) of that initial encounter with then Captain Chapman. I didn't know him, but intuition told me that this was a guy that I would follow into the jaws of hell. Which I did, but fortunately along the way we became friends also. This Marine's Marine definitely affected my standards as to what a Marine is all about.

30

Chapter 9   November 22, 1963

Most Americans remember that date, at least those of my generation and those who came before me. It seems that many of the youth of this nation don't have an appreciation for history. November 22, 1963, stands as a monumental date for me, much in the same vein that December 7, 1941 (Pearl Harbor), and June 6, 1944 (D-Day), did for my predecessors in knowing and being affected by significant dates, events, or people. The same may hold true for some for April 14, 1865, the day of the first presidential assassination when Abraham Lincoln was shot at age fifty-six (see Chapter 2; How's that for another irony?). Perhaps, however, I'm getting carried away with having been a history major in my liberal arts education.

I think John F. Kennedy affected people in this country and abroad, one way or another, to such a degree that this date is indelible in our respective minds. It may have been his whole Camelot aura, his undefinable charisma, his engaging public personality, his apparent sincerity about his (almost mine) generation moving this country forward, his family values and ties, his youth and vigor when compared to the previous political administrations, his image as "American royalty," his approach to civil liberties, or even his social shenanigans (as we learned about later on). Or it may have simply been, as with me, the tragic fact that he was an American President who was assassinated in his prime.

The 1960s were a turbulent time. If it wasn't the Vietnam war that polarized you, it may have been your conservative or liberal approach/reaction to JFK's and RFK's perspectives and actions toward the civil rights movement, or it could have been any of the myriad issues of the day that had a bearing on your feelings about November 22, 1963. No matter what your politics were, most people were shocked, dismayed, and genuinely saddened by President Kennedy's death, probably more so because of the means of his death than anything else.

In the sixties, I was a military man. We had freedom of choice just like any citizen. We were discouraged from actively participating in any political endeavor or cause, however. I had two tours in Vietnam as a helicopter pilot. I saw my share of death and I lost a couple of buddies. I also witnessed the public anti-war uprising that so divisively splintered this country. Since I lived and worked in the military environment, which can be quite insulated from the civilian world, I didn't have a full appreciation for the anti-war perspective. It is true that I grew to be disillusioned about the reasons for our involvement in a civil war a million miles from our shores - it was a politically rather than a military controlled war - but I had a job to do and I did it. No questions asked. Some may describe that as unquestionable obedience, but that's the nature of the military, certainly the Marine Corps.

I had recently returned home from my first tour in Nam, being assigned to Quantico, VA. My R&D (Research and Development) staff job negated a lot of flying time. I say that because on November 22, 1963 I happened to be on a flight between Quantico and Grumman Bethpage in Long Island, NY to visit a vendor with whom I was working on a new project. To pass the time in the air, we had our AM radio on. And then the "flash" announcement came over the airways -

President Kennedy had been shot. My co-pilot and I were stunned. Upon arrival at our destination, we were informed that our Commander-in-Chief had died from his wounds. To say the least, it was difficult for us to continue with our mission. but we did; that's what we were paid for. The impact of that news wasn't personal of course. but it was after all, regardless of our individual political beliefs, our Commander-in-Chief who had been killed. That almost translates, to a military man, that we had lost our leader, a fellow comrade in arms. That can be very traumatic.

The comprehensiveness of the assassination was graphically enhanced by the funeral procession a few days later. The military aspect of the event struck me hard emotionally, for Kennedy was a comrade-in-arms. I was glued to the TV for I guess the entire elongated event, from the public viewing of the casket, to John-John's salute, to the parade march to Arlington National Cemetery, and finally to the lighting of the eternal flame. My eyes were not dry for those many hours of screen viewing. It was a most sad occasion, which for me as a military "pomp-and-circumstances" appreciator doubled the impact of the funeral process. The reversed boots on that black stallion, symbolizing the "downed" commander, was an added extra emphasis toward creating an air of loss.

The subsequent fiasco of the Oswald handling and the hysteria of the conspiracy theories were side-shows to the actual assassination and funeral, at least for me. It seemed that this country had suffered a great loss. In retrospect, many Americans lives may have been saved if the speculation was true that JFK was about to withdraw from the Vietnam quagmire. Who knows how history may have been altered if Kennedy had lived and served another term in the White House. Being a Kennedy clan fan, if you will, I think we would have seen a more positive world. His impact and potential remain a question, but a very bright scenario that was not to be realized. He and his death touched me. I like to think that we all would have been better off without the fall of this modern-day Camelot.

Chapter 10   The Adoption Of My Son Jeff

My wife Pat and I decided that we would practice birth control for the first year or so of our marriage. After all, I was still in flight school (if I flunked out, I would lose my "flight skins" - extra compensation for being on flight status - upon reverting to a "ground-pounder" - a Marine infantry Officer), so making ends meet was always a challenge. We also wisely concluded that we should learn more about each other before bringing a new face into the relationship. Of additional consideration from my end was the fact that I wasn't really ready to become a father. I immediately, and correctly, deduced that I wanted to "play" for a while before I took on the responsibilities of fatherhood.

The first year passed, as did three plus more. No pregnancy. We were actively trying for a baby, although a thirteen-month tour overseas interrupted physical contact. We were now stationed in Quantico, VA and I had a great job in an R&D (Research & Development) environment. Admittedly, I still preferred our life to be just the two of us. But Pat felt the biological clock ticking. We had ourselves medically checked out to determine why we weren't conceiving. There were apparently no medical complications for either of us in that vein. A mystery of life! Pat initially explored on her own the possibility of adoption. When she raised the issue to me, I resisted. Raising someone else's kid!? Not for me, or so I thought. I finally succumbed to Pat's insistence, recognizing that not moving the family concept forward would pose a chasm between us.

We decided to use the services of the Children's Home Society, a non-profit (as I recall) private entity (as opposed to a governmental agency). They were terrific people to deal with. Definitely understanding of the potential adopting parents' mind-sets and emotional considerations. I was still hesitant, and probably showed it. The day finally arrived for us to observe the prospective baby and review its history and medical situation.

The first baby they asked us to consider had some sort of medical problem (I don't recall the specifics). Because I was in the military with free medical services available to me and my family, they projected that the costs of correcting the physical deficiency would be negligible. That would have been true, but after careful consideration, Pat and I mutually declined that baby. We invoked the philosophy that if we had to have children through adoption, we might as well be choosy.

Christmas with Michelle and Jeff—
he still has a love for aviation.

33

The day arrived soon afterwards that they had another baby that matched our ethnic background and medical requirements. As we met to review his (we didn't care about gender) history, we observed the cutest bundle of joy, who instantaneously captured our hearts. What a change in me. My attitude about having children and this whole adoption process took a 180 degree turn. I distinctly remember the day that we signed the papers and retrieved the baby. We were both nervous, as I suppose any first-time parent (biological or adoptive) would be. Pat carried Jeff home, while I drove. After deliberation, we decided on Jeffrey for a name, along with Drummond - my father's middle name and apparently a family moniker - for a middle name. As soon as I cradled him in my arms for the first time, I knew I had done the right thing. I wasn't sure I wanted to be a father right up to that moment, but it all changed in a flash. What pride I had! It was truly a magnificent feeling of oneness. The adoption facet was immaterial. He was mine - "my man," as I came to call him through the years. No father could have had a more powerful innate feeling of joy. I suppose my pride was not unique, given that all (or at least most) fathers have similar feelings. But for me, a person who was not crazy about being tied to a family, the change in attitude was monumental. I loved it. I loved him. I loved Pat for suggesting this route. And I loved me for feeling this way. The affect of being a new papa still brings chills of remembrance to my very soul.

Author with son, Jeff, 1990.

Chapter 11 My Daughter Michelle's Maturation

This chapter is a bit out of sequence in the chronology of the significant events of my life. But I wanted to couple Michelle's entry and subsequent trials and tribulations with the same context as the preceding chapter.

Mich-Mash, as I affectionately call her (she was named after the Beatles'song), is also adopted. But she is not related to Jeff biologically. Pat and I decided that after four years of raising one child, we needed to expand the family. By now (1968-70), I was stationed at Camp Pendleton, CA as the Officer-in-Charge of the airfield at that major grunt facility. In those days, it was a single squadron base with support functions of such things as Airfield Operations, Crash Crew, Meteorology, Fuel Farm, Air Traffic Control, and base security and maintenance, all of which were my responsibility. That airfield has expanded considerably since my departure from the Marine Corps in 1970; it's now a full MAG (Marine Air Group), with further expansion scheduled due to the recent (vintage mid-1990s) military base re-alignment and closures.

The adoption process was similar to Jeff's, although we obtained her through the San Diego County Welfare Department. The same feelings of pride blossomed in me. Perhaps the event itself wasn't as startling for me, as it was the second time around (no offense, Michelle). And we certainly welcomed this new bundle of joy into our home with the same love, resolution of joy, and unbridled merriment as we had with Jeff. We had a little girl now, and, like a father having a son, it was a special event.

But that is not the theme of this chapter. Instead I want to talk about the maturation process that Michelle went through. That in itself, finalized by me "walking her down the aisle" (I'm getting ahead of myself), is the culmination of perhaps a miraculous turnaround that I was dubious about ever seeing.

Michelle had the unfortunate reality of being a victim of Pat's and my divorce (as was Jeff, in a different manner, which could be the subject of another chapter, or even a separate book). She was only three when I departed the scene. Hardly enough time for us to really get to know each other, especially given that the last year or so was a tenuous family situation because of the problems Pat and I were having.

Daughter Michelle
hams it up for Dad.

Following the divorce, Michelle was re-introduced to me via the summer visitation routine. Granted, I had her come to my new bachelor pad in Hermosa Beach with Jeff the very next summer (1973) after the geographic separation, so there was no major time loss, except that it was a summer visitation routine in which I spoiled the kids (typical for the estranged father, isn't it?) That certainly is not the same (for either child) as being in a family setting. Anyway, to abbreviate this chapter, let it suffice to say that the summer and alternate Christmas visitations were special for me (and hopefully for them), and I did as good a job as I could in instilling a sense of long-distance "family" to alleviate my misconceptions of not being wanted.

Mich came to live with me at age fifteen (Jeff had done so at age eleven). She, like Jeff, was experiencing some problems with Pat. I, of course, welcomed the opportunity to have Michelle with me. Jeff by now was off on his own, and I was going through the agonies of a relationship breakdown (see Chapter 21). I quickly learned that my little girl, who was probably going through her own agonies of self-realization, had acquired a drug problem. Pat had unsuccessfully combated that anomaly in her own way. Not that I was much help. Mich knew I was still a cop, having left the FBI and entered the corporate security world. She probably viewed me as the enemy, thought I had no understanding or tolerance to drug usage (not so to the former; yes to the latter), and was not empathetic to her growing pains (which was untrue). I watched Mich's behavior degenerate to reclusiveness and truancy. Not that she was a "rotten kid;" she wasn't. She just needed to learn the hard way who her friends really were and what was the best path for her growth. It finally became a revelation to her when she acquired a new boy friend (at age 18), a college student who aspired to become a Naval Aviator (how's that for irony?). He was adamant about a no-drugs life style, and she complied. Man, did I welcome him into her life. He (named Jeff, also an irony since she and her brother did not like each other) really squared her away, but unfortunately became either too possessive or too "square" for Michelle (I'm not sure I know the real reason). Her Jeff was gone, but his influence - thankfully - sustained. Even though she immediately acquired a somewhat "spaced out" (in my unknowledgeable opinion) new boyfriend, she was on her way toward being drug free (for the most part, if you don't count occasional use of marijuana, I guess).

Michelle and Misty loved the water, a typical summer visitation scene.

With Michelle now living in San Jose (I had a two year stint working there) and me having returned to Southern California, she was really on her own at age eighteen-nineteen. She informed me that she was moving to Fort Lauderdale, FL with her new boyfriend, who was to be financed through school by his father there. A short time thereafter, she advised me that the father had reneged on the housing he had promised them, and the boyfriend, named Casey, sided with the father regarding her status in that picture. So she moved a couple of thousand miles only to be stranded. Fortunately, her homelessness didn't reach the critical stage, as she met and fell in love with someone she was working with. I was confident that Mich's experience with the male counterpart gave her enough smarts to deal realistically with her relationships. She told me all about Rob Biggar, including their plans for marriage. WOW! Was that quick, or what?

Moving this story forward a few months, in late February 1994, my second daughter Misty (see Chapter 20) and I flew to Ft. Lauderdale for the wedding. I had only spoken to Rob once on the phone, and he really impressed me. Talk about old-fashioned values in asking the father permission for the daughter's hand in marriage. Rob called me a couple of days before Valentine's Day the year before, informing me of his plans to "pop the question" to Mich on V-day 1993. "Inform" isn't really the right word. Although I'm sure he would still have proposed if I said "no" to his request, he showed me a lot of class by asking for my blessings. I didn't have to require a personal meeting before giving my blessings. Between Mich's description (as well as Pat's) and his demeanor during our one telephone conversation, I knew he was the guy for Mich.

One of my most proud moments—
walking Michelle down the aisle.

The day of the marriage (February 25, 1994) arrived. Misty and I had arrived a few days earlier, so we were a part of the ceremony practice and other social activities. When I finally met Rob soon after Mich met us at the airport, I quickly was reassured that this was one squared-away guy. She couldn't have done better. We all anxiously watched the weather, as they had planned and practiced for an outdoor event at a local country club. It was beautiful weather for the preceding days, but, alas, on February 25, 1994 the rain came. No anguish, however, as the back-up plans brought them inside without too much disappointment.

So here I was - the father of the bride. As I waited for Mich to make her appearance to walk down the aisle with me, I reflected back on her struggle to find herself. She had beaten the odds regarding getting off the drugs, she had become an independent and dependable young lady with physical beauty to match, and she had found happiness with a young man who has great potential vocationally, as well as for cementing the relationship. I could see and feel the love they had for each other. It was contagious. I wish I could have shared that joy with Pat (she was there with her husband), but unfortunately she felt the pressure of his (the husband) hesitancy to have any liaison with me. It would have been nice to have shared a few memories with Pat.

It was time. The band (actually a string trio, as I recall) began "Here Comes The Bride." The dressing room door opened and there was my lovely Mich-Mash in all her glory. I was overwhelmed. Instant tears of joy flooded my eyes (I think Mich had one or two also). I presented her with a rose (as I did for her mother when we reached the end of the aisle), put her arm in mine, and proudly stepped forward to meet the awaiting throng. It was a short walk, but an eternity of swelling pride, love, and a feeling of accomplishment for me (OK, I'm taking some credit for helping her to this stage). It was a "passing of the guard," as I reflected back on the wedding Pat and I had. Hopefully, Rob and Mich won't make the mistakes Pat and I made. I have full confidence in them both that they'll have a long and happy journey together.

Michelle and Rob Biggar
on their wedding day.

Chapter 12   June 30, 1970

A career change, to say the very least. I don't care how many years a military person devotes to his/her country, it's still a tough transition to the civilian world. Granted, it's more difficult attitudinally for someone with twenty-plus years in the service than for a one-tour enlisted person (e.g., two-four years). I put in eleven years; I wanted to do twenty for retirement benefits purposes, as I've previously stated. The transition was horrendous for me, and it certainly affected my perspective on many things, as I look back now after twenty-six years as a civilian.

To quote an old adage: "Confession is good for the soul." I think it's time for me to "fess up" about my departure from the Marine Corps. For personal pride and professional advancement reasons, I have been proclaiming a half-truth about my "resignation." In short, my departure wasn't because I had to voluntarily choose between career and family. I was the victim of a "RIF" (Reduction In Force). That doesn't sound like a big deal these days, given the rash of corporate and military "downsizing," "right-sizing," or "RIFs" that are so prevalent. There is no stigma being "laid-off" nowadays; in 1970 it was different.

Let me provide some mitigating and extenuating circumstances, which may sound like a cop-out, but in actuality had a tremendous being on my transition.

Elsewhere in this book, I have documented that I had returned from my second tour in Viet Nam in July 1968. Disembarking from the aircraft that took me from DaNang to El Toro, I was greeted by a very chilling wife (Pat - number one in my chain). A couple of hours later she advised me that she wanted a divorce, or at least a trial separation for a while. Welcome home, Marine! Not exactly what I expected.

Author as USMC helicopter pilot.

To abbreviate the sequence of events and conversations, for the next two years, during my assignment as the officer-in-charge of the airfield at Camp Pendleton, Pat and I (after we reconciled) discussed the merits of our potential together, the affects that the Marine Corps would have on our relationship and family status/structure, and the opportunities that might be available to me in the civilian world. These discussions were expedited near the end of my first year at Camp Pendleton when I learned that I had been "passed over" for the rank of permanent Major.

During the Viet Nam war, promotions came quickly (typical in wartime). After only three years as a captain (normally in the Marine Corps, which is the slowest of all services to promote, it takes about seven years to make Major), I was promoted to "temporary" Major, meaning that I had to be affirmed by Headquarters Marine Corps the next year for "permanent" Major. Because I had an unusual split-tour in Nam (see below) and a rather unique three plus year assignment in an R&D environment at Quantico, in which I was instrumental in the development and acquisition of innovative aviation equipment into the Marine Corps' inventory, I figured I was a shoe-in for the "permanent" rank.

When the promotion list came out, I was aghast! I actually thought there was a misprint. Determining that was not the case, I requested and received copies of my fitness reports from day one. I discovered that my commanding officer, during my assignment as the provost marshal and company commander for perimeter defense for MCAF Marble Mountain adjacent to DaNang, had given me what was termed a "marginal" fitness report. All my other evaluations, especially in my R&D assignment, were graded "outstanding". In those days, a marginal fitness report in a combat environment was a killer, almost a guarantee that your career will be abbreviated. I thought it unfair, primarily because I was given an assignment outside of my "MOS (Military Occupational Specialty). Mine was that of a helicopter pilot. Normally, that type of ground defense and police specialist is given to a "ground-pounder" officer. I hadn't even been to the Infantry Officers Basic School (I went directly from OCS to Naval Flight School), so I wasn't thoroughly trained to do the job. But we're all Marines first (aviators second), and we're expected to do the grunt job regardless. I thought my five-month split tour in that capacity was performed in more than a satisfactory manner, but it was my boss' call.

In order to be "RIFed," an officer had to receive two consecutive "pass-overs." In all of my naiveté, I never thought that would happen to me. So I didn't take any action to negate that possibility. I could easily have received a glowing "Special Fitness Report" from my boss at El Toro who had oversight over the Camp Pendleton airfield. That in itself could have done the trick. I also could have written a personal request for a "special" from the Assistant Commandant of the Marine Corps - a four-star General by the name of Lew Walt. He had been the Commanding General of the Development Center at Quantico as a one-star when I was at that R&D facility a few years earlier. I am confident that he would have provided that "Special Fitness Report," or even gone to greater lengths to influence the promotion board. But, alas, I did neither. Part of the reason I declined to ask for those special evaluations was pride (I wanted the promotion on my own merit), and part of it was due to Pat's influence on me to leave the Corps. I could have negated the latter influence, but I didn't. If the marriage was going to work, which I wanted, she would not have been happy with me leaving her and the two kids every three or four years for another combat tour (the war was still hot-and-heavy).

My somewhat nihilistic approach of doing nothing to interdict the promotion board resulted in my second pass-over. The die was now cast. I was scheduled to depart the Marine Corps on June 30, 1970. I had plenty of time to seek out new employment, but in those days I was not as astute in that activity as I am today. I had no ambition to fly for the airlines. I did pursue opportunities in airport management, but I quickly learned, after visiting with every airport manager in Southern

California, that the field was very narrow. One had to start at a starvation salary in "East Podunk" somewhere. I had a family to support and wanted to stay in Southern California, if I could.

Author (#10) tipping in basket at All-Marine Basketball Tournament

No need to expend ink on the hows and whys of my easy transition to the FBI; that's not the purpose of this chapter. The effect that my discharge date of June 30, 1970 had on me is the theme of this writing.

I was warned that taking off the uniform would be difficult. It was.

The best years of my life were devoted to the Marine Corps and all it stood for - I still adhere to that perspective, even after twenty-six years of interesting times in the FBI, corporate security management, and outplacement services. I was definitely indoctrinated by my recruiter, during OCS, and by my experiences in combat and "garrison" ("stateside," for you civilians). Indoctrinated in the most favorable of connotations.

During my days as a Marine Corps officer, the Corps had a few advertising mottoes, namely: "The Marine Corps Builds Men," "The Marine Corps Is Looking For A Few Good Men," and "The Few; The Proud; The Marines." Anyone can decipher the elitism and pride that's innate to those mottoes. Almost all active duty and former officers and most enlisted Marines also subscribe to our other motto: "Once A Marine, Always A Marine." The sense of camaraderie and esprit de corps that you learn, accept, and proclaim are unique to the Marine Corps. No other service even approaches that breeding, and in my experience I know of no corporate entity that projects that bonding to its personnel or to the public. It just doesn't exist. The profit motive and "ladder-climbing" suppresses a commonality that is pervasively necessary for camaraderie. The FBI (and perhaps some other federal governmental agencies) tried to duplicate that image (In fact, J. Edgar Hoover encouraged the recruitment of former Marines - and Mormons; how's that for a dichotomy?!), but it was a false image, as I was to learn. There were dedicated disciples of Hoover, but the Bureau's policies were perpetuated on his 1930s reputation and were not modernized to incorporate a more sophisticated recruit or the modern management techniques developed by experts (e.g., McGregor; Maslow; Skinner; Likert; Argyris; Herzberg; Drucker) in that field.

I cried in my beer (actually, rum-and-cokes were my standard) the evening of June 30, 1970 after I received my DD214 and other discharge papers. I didn't even go to the Officer's Club for a final drink. I immediately felt the impact of being on the outside. No longer was I one of the "finest fighting machine in the world." I was a stranger in a strange land. An outcast, to boot. My eleven years went for naught. No retirement benefits; no rights to the "O" Club, commissary or PX, or free medical services; no more salutes - given or taken; no more proudly wearing of the uniforms that meant so much to me; no more of the joys of flying helicopters; no more happy hours with people of similar backgrounds and experiences; no more immediate potential for the respect gained from advanced rank; no more innate camaraderie and esprit de corps to augment that special feeling of belonging.

It was a difficult, sad, and demeaning day. I still have not recovered from that loss. I have never learned how to "let go" of that love, and I don't want to. I was and am still foremost a Marine, if not now in actuality, at least in spirit. That will never change. And I'm proud of that. Semper Fi!!!

Author receiving Air Medal award in 1964 from Brigadier General Lew Walt, with first wife, Pat, looking on.

Author flying in formation of H-34 helicopters off coast of Viet Nam in 1962

Author in front of his UH-1E during 2nd Viet Nam tour, 1967-68

Chapter 13 Suzanne And The FBI

I choose to devote a brief chapter to this young lady, not as a slap in the face to my first wife, Pat, but as a reminder to me of how special that feeling of "love" can be, no matter what the outcome. I apologize to Pat for documenting this, but I believe that Suzanne (again, last name deleted for discretionary reasons) had such an effect on me to prompt her inclusion herein.

My two year tenure with the FBI as a special agent, following my departure from the Marine Corps, found me first in Washington, D.C. and Quantico, VA for training, in Seattle, WA for my first year in the field, and then down I-5 to Portland, OR for my next assignment. Pat ostensibly stayed behind in Seattle to finish her master's degree work at the University of Washington, but I suspected that she was preparing for the inevitable divorce. We really had done nothing to solidify our relationship or correct the basic problems that led us to this almost irreversible junction of separation. We separated for three months at Camp Pendleton when I returned from my second tour in Nam, but only reconciled - I think - as a matter of convenience (or guilt, given the circumstances, which I won't get into). No therapy, no real communication, no remedial inner examinations. So divorce was inevitable.

When I arrived in Portland, I met Suzanne, who was the secretary to one of our supervisors. How convenient, or inconvenient (depending on discretion). It proved to be disastrously inconvenient, however, as this intra-office affair, especially in view of the Bureau's policies in those days, proved not viably realistic for continuance, even after Pat said "sayonara."

Suzanne, who was about twelve years my junior, was a gorgeous and sparkling firebird. Of all the women I have known through subsequent years, she was the epitome of a siren seductress. When she targeted me, I was flattered, apprehensive, and excited. It was dangerous to be involved in an intra-office affair. Pat and I also had not yet finalized our leaning toward divorce. So I entered this "friendship" with Suzanne cautiously. Needless to say, I was unsuccessful in maintaining proper decorum. I was seduced. The "animal attraction," which is a quaint and really derogatory expression for a strong magnetic physical attraction, prevailed. I couldn't resist her charm, the spirit of adventure that she posed, and that "special" (another overused word) feeling of emotional bonding that I felt. Perhaps the timing was right for me to reaffirm my own personal attractiveness to a "sweet young thing." That "timing" was disastrous, however, as our efforts to make this affair a clandestine one backfired. Perhaps it was that time of my life that I needed to "sow my oats," regardless of the people involved who could be hurt. Or perhaps I again truly experienced that joy of love that had diminished in my marriage. Whatever the reason, I let it happen.

For about six months, Suzanne and I carried on an exciting affair that was full of the qualities which describe a "magnificent obsession." Physically and emotionally it surpassed anything that Pat and I had. It was an awakening for me. I suppose that's as good a reason as any to stray from a marriage (or is that a cop out?). We shared some wonderful times together, full of physical plenty, as well as communicative importance. The "affair" rapidly moved from "extra-curricular" to plans for permanence. There is no need to cite herein examples of reasons for the progression.

As a means of summation, Suzanne re-invigorated my lust for life.

But here's the irony. For whatever reason - a strong sense of responsibility I believe - I told Suzanne that I needed to try one last time to make my marriage to Pat work. That was a devastating conversation. I subsequently learned that Suzanne suffered a breakdown immediately thereafter. Visiting her in the hospital reaffirmed my love for her, but unfortunately aggravated her mother. Now the "cat was out of the bag." Suzanne's mother became a "whistle-blower." The subsequent Bureau investigation concerning allegations of impropriety led to the demise of my career with that organization, my relationship with Suzanne, and my marriage to Pat. Some readers may say I deserved the outcome, which may have merit. I do not know of many human beings who could resist the temptations of love that Suzanne and I felt, however. Regardless of the irresponsibility concerning my desertion of my marriage and family. I'm not especially proud of my actions in retrospect (I am a bit older and wiser these days), but I could not help myself then. Suzanne had that effect on me.

She opened my eyes and heart to a new level of love. For that, I thank her. Her effect had to be documented in this life story.

Chapter 14 Arlene: My Guru

Leaving the comfort of the military, with a brief tenure in the Bureau, and a marriage that failed because of ignorance of interpersonal relations (which includes knowledge of what makes a marriage work) was a traumatic experience. Fortunately, I had smarts enough to seek out therapy as soon as I got myself situated in Hermosa Beach and Hughes Aircraft Company. An enormous and most influential co-stimulator was an extraordinary woman by the name of Arlene. She was to become my "guru," as I called her, in matters pertaining to my initial growth and expansion into the enlightening realm of self-improvement.

Before I settled in Hermosa Beach, I briefly looked to San Diego as my location of preference. Initially taking an apartment in that southern most California city. I re-contracted an outplacement services firm that had helped me formulate a resume upon my discharge from the Marine Corps. At the receptionist's desk sat Arlene, her long jet black hair, statuesque body, and sultry voice beckoning me to make this more than a professional visit. She was a magnificent example of feminine pulchritude. I was soon to learn that she also was a knowledgeable and esoteric practitioner of self-actualization techniques, especially from the Far Eastern philosophical ideologies and practices. I had studied oriental religions and philosophies years before at college and prior to my first overseas assignment, so my attraction to Arlene's projections was a natural.

Since I was now open to learning the intricacies of interpersonal relations and self-improvement, my relationship with Arlene became that of a two-edged sword. but for me both blades being of a positive nature. We dated and became physically involved, which was more than nice. More importantly, she led me into arenas that were virgin territory for me, intellectually and spiritually. Again, I won't expound on the details of this enlightenment, for the things I learned are not the focus of this material. By taking me into an appreciation for nature. for non-Christian values, and for demonstrative actions with fellow human beings, Arlene was probably the initiator of my growth and inquisitiveness into the teachings of modern proponents/advocates of self-improvement. If it had not been for Arlene, I probably would not have later been receptive to Fritz Pearl's Gestalt Theory, Eric Frohm's "The Art of Loving." Maxwell Maltz's "Psychocybernetics," Og Mandino's miracles books (e.g., "The Greatest Miracle In The World"), the many other authors who proclaimed the fundamentals of self-improvement, and even to Tony Robbins' "Unlimited Power" and "Awaken The Giant Within." They all have contributed to me becoming a more complete person, someone Pat certainly wouldn't recognize as being her former husband. I attribute my growth to the stimulus provided by that exceptional woman of this chapter who took me under her wing.

An interesting postscript to my relationship with Arlene occurred twelve years later. Our initial coupling faded once I moved to Hermosa Beach and began my multiple dating mode. After all, Arlene was by then "g.u." ("geographically undesirable," an unflattering beach people connotation which reflected the vast availability of eligible potential mates in the immediate locale). How parochial and trendy is that? My loss is one way, but I had to get the mass dating thing out of my system before moving on.

Anyway, twelve years after my initial encounter with Arlene, I happened to be in a local donut shop in San Diego getting the morning gut-bombs for my troops at General Dynamics. As I casually looked to my side at the tall blond next to me, I had to do a double-take. "Arlene?" I asked, almost unbelieving. I almost did not recognize her, as the jet black long hair was now blond, and strikingly so, much in the same vein as was her original shade twelve years earlier. Her later explanation copped-out to "blondes have more fun." So we re-established liaison, much in the same manner as before. I admit feeling a bit guilty about it. Dona (see Chapter 21) and I were still seeing each other, although the chasm between us was getting larger and larger. Sorry, Dona, I never told you about Arlene; no sense in aggravating our already tenuous situation. I still loved Dona, but the temptation that Arlene posed was just too much. That liaison didn't last long, primarily because of my feelings for Dona. But it was an interesting follow-up to our prior relationship. And come to think of it, as of this writing another twelve years have passed. Arlene and I used to joke about that every twelve years reunion potential. I wonder if she's still in town?

Chapter 15 The Gallery And Wayne Bradshaw

I was no stranger to partying. The Marine Corps has the reputation of "working hard and playing hard." I had more than my share of social activities during my eleven years as a marine officer and pilot. Between Friday evening happy hours (no civilian females allowed!) at stateside officers clubs, a steady flow of libations in Nam, and other organizational and personal functions within the Marine Corps framework, my participation in the "party" scene was considerable. I also had some collegiate experience - the typical beer drinking and fraternity "toga" parties (As I recall, I don't believe we ever did the actual toga bit). I never had the opportunity, however, to indulge in an adult bachelorhood, having been married right out of college. So I missed that aspect of "growing up" that usually fills the life of someone in their twenties and early thirties.

Man, did I ever make up for that deficiency following my first divorce! I had an excellent taste of military sociability, but I knew that it had to be different in the civilian world, even though I was approaching this bachelorhood in my mid to late thirties. I also knew where I wanted to test those social waters. As the Beach Boys song goes, "There's nothing like a California girl!"

Being familiar with Southern California from my days in the Corps, I knew that was the site for me. As I left the drizzle of the Pacific Northwest ("Northwet" was the popular colloquialism), I envisioned a period of social interactions on the sunny beaches (and associated party spots) of Southern California. My first choice was San Diego, but I was not adverse to Orange County or even the Los Angeles basin. I also planned on living in a large apartment complex in a coastal city in order to facilitate the "laid-back," shorts, and T-shirts social mixing.

I was not displeased with the results. Since my new job as a security Investigator for Hughes Aircraft Company, doing essentially the same thing I did in the Bureau but within the confines of that company, had me officed near LAX (Los Angeles International Airport), I concentrated my apartment search in El Segundo, Manhattan Beach, Hermosa Beach, and Redondo Beach (north to south from LAX). As luck would have it, one of the first places I looked at was a third floor loft in a complex called "The Gallery" in Hermosa Beach. It was two blocks from "The Strand" (the walkway that borders the beach, which for me at the time was cost prohibitive to live on). I looked at other places after viewing that well-situated apartment and complex, but I quickly gravitated back to The Gallery. Apartment #351 was mine. Timing is everything they say, as that loft was the last one available (I didn't care for the standard one or two bedroom boxes that was typical of all other apartments, and I didn't want someone living above me due to the noise factor).

I didn't crank up my social feelers immediately. I mentioned in previous chapters that I wanted to seek out some therapy/counseling first. I needed to learn considerably more about myself and interpersonal relations before I went "on the prowl." During the first couple of months, I was somewhat of a recluse, spending most of my free evenings reading. The pool and spa, with its throngs of people gathered about them did indeed beckon to me (especially on weekends), but I resisted. Finally, a neighbor of mine (Wayne Bradshaw) introduced himself, became impressed with my FBI background, and then led me to the pool. The first introductions were polite and non-chalant, as most first meetings are. But Wayne is a catalyst. Out came the frozen daiquiris. That was to become a Gallery pool-side attraction. And more! Soon I had met and established a rapport with almost every partier at The Gallery. We became known as "the group," a contingent of ten-fifteen regular activists in the social swirl. Its cast of characters were diverse, but we all seemed to hit it off well together. Very few dated within "the group," so that sort of competition didn't exist or prove to be a wedge in our social circle.

Our activities were also diverse. We had innumerable pool/spa impromptu gatherings, which included pool volleyball. At times we would take the party to the nearby beach or to someone's apartment (People from an adjacent complex - where Candy lived - would sometimes come over). Such was our reputation for merriment! We would also organize special event parties (e.g., Cinco de Mayo; Renaissance Faire; Busch Gardens; a rotating soup night at our respective apartments; brunch at a local restaurant; street fairs; or any place where party diversity would encourage the use of alcohol, the perpetuation of laughter, and the potential for impressing a date - or prospect). We never had anything like this in the Marine Corps. It's what I missed as a young adult, and I took full advantage of that lifestyle.

Wayne Bradshaw, seated on left, at some Gallery function.

I think I should insert here the extent of my regard for Wayne Bradshaw. He was, as mentioned, the catalyst for my initial introductions to "the group." He became more than that, much more. Of the male cast of the group, there were primarily three central figures in my activities. There was Wayne, with the classic salesman attitude and demeanor, who eventually built a very successful independent insurance business head-quartered in Redondo Beach from The Gallery days of being a recent transplant from his native Norfolk, VA - via a couple of jobs in New York City and thereabouts. Secondly, there was Simeon Davis, an active duty United States Air Force captain, pilot, and engineer, who like Wayne was a "redneck" southerner (from NC) -sorry, guys, this Yankee author has to stick it to you rebs every so often to remind you of who won the war. And finally there was Dana Skulsky, a twenty-four-year-old recent graduate from Oregon State (or was it Oregon University?; I always get those confused, especially since my Marine Corps friend Jack Palmer - see Chapter 17 - was from the other school), whose gregarious personality usually attracted the group to his apartment for libations. All three were congenial people, but each had his own style. Dana, as a young man right out of college with a water polo background, charmed the ladies and popularized the perpetuating party scene. Simeon was more conservative and commanded respect by example and proper decorum. I obviously related to him, because of our mutual military and aviation orientation, in a much different way than to my other new-found civilian friends. Wayne, on the other hand, was a unique character. I never have had the pleasure of knowing someone, on other than a casual or professional basis, who exuded the mastery of a convincing, positive, and energetic approach to almost anything - a natural born salesman, as I call that type. Wayne, like both Dana and Simeon, could charm his way into anybody's life, but in a much more controlling manner (which is not meant to be a negative connotation). Wayne was THE social organizer at The Gallery. He also became the true friend who would give me (or almost anyone) the proverbial shirt off his back, as he demonstrated to me during my times of need.

Before moving on to other Gallery thoughts, I'd like to touch on how Wayne and I survived the inevitability of the break-up of "the group." The group sort of fell apart as an all-encompassing social whirl when most of us splintered into different life-styles. I married Candy and moved to Manhattan Beach. Wayne and Simeon also married, the former purchasing a townhouse kitty-cornered to The Gallery (as did Dana at about the same time), while Simeon was shortly thereafter transferred to an Air Force Base outside of the Los Angeles basin. I never saw Wayne or Dana much thereafter, except for a traditional Christmas party at the latter's pad. On a couple of occasions I visited Wayne, at times with my son Jeff, but Wayne's continuous beach life-style in his hot tub turned to bare-bottomed romps and (as I understand it, not having been there) group orgies, which was an uncomfortable scene for me with my eleven-year-old son (I stumbled onto that scene once with Jeff). So that potential scene limited my liaison with Wayne. Our friendship became further estranged after I left the beach (with Candy leaving a year before), got involved with Dona, and moved to Orange County. For whatever reason, we never fully continued the close liaison thereafter, including during my two-year stint in San Jose following the demise of Dona's and my nine-year relationship.

True friendship never dies, no matter the passage of time or the separation of distance. I think Wayne and I both recognized that in our different ways. An illustration of the sincerity of the rooted friendship from The Gallery days occurred upon my return to Southern California from San Jose in 1989. Wayne invited me to camp out at his home (now in Redondo Beach) while I house and job hunted. As a precipitation to that arrangement, we had what I considered to be the single most honest and entrenching conversation I've ever had concerning the reasons for our estrangement and perceived alienation. This forthright revelation did not bring up any substantial negative responses to our respective views, as I thought it might. Instead, I found the conversation cleansing, enlightening, and cohesive to the extent of it confirming that we were indeed friends, no matter what had transpired during the previous ten or so years. During my month's stay at Wayne's place (he was not married at the time, having just terminated a live-in relationship and having also met his soon-to-be bride Kelly, a lovely, lively, and gracious redhead of an Irish heritage, with whom I have thoroughly enjoyed a kindredship since their marriage).

From that date forward (May '89), Wayne and I re-established the type of friendship that I so cherish. It is now more than just based on the commonality of the party scene. He has been there for me during K.C.'s and my divorce, during my times of need for conversation (usually over a pitcher of daiquiris or margaritas), and even now as I fight this cancer of mine and try to provide a financial base for my grown children. Perhaps I should have written a separate chapter on Wayne, but I think this coupling of The Gallery scene to Wayne's enormous and indelible impression on my civilian life fits together quite well in illustrating the importance of the inception of the friendship to its current stage of being a solid male bonding relationship.

Getting off that tangent, let me return to The Gallery side of this chapter by saying that there are all sorts of vignettes that I could develop into interesting and amusing anecdotes. Of the many, many stories, I'm not sure which ones I would select as illustrations of my social involvement. Again, that's not the purpose of this chapter or book. How did that Bachelorhood affect my life? Several ways.

I am a social animal by nature, always have been and ..... (oops, I was going to say "always will be," but my present medical situation has a bearing on that future). In the formation of my persona/character/self/psyche, I recognized that I needed a Bachelorhood to somewhat complete my development (much in the same vein as I needed to expand in the self-improvement arena). My early marriage disrupted what I, in retrospect, perceived to be the normal flow cycle for a social animal. Perhaps that's one reason for my subconscious marital discontent, especially during the later stages of my first marriage. Well, I did the bachelor bit to the hilt, and I did it in an environment of my choosing. It didn't last long; it didn't have to. By the time I settled in with Candy, I knew that I had gotten that partying out of my system. I didn't totally lose interest in social interactions - I never will. But to do what I did was quite sufficient to get me back on track to move my development forward.

In conjunction with partying - which I'll put in the context of alcoholic merriment - I also needed to have the flexibility of being involved with many women. Now, I'm no Wilt Chamberlain (in basketball prowess and in his self-professed conquests of women), but I did my share of dating, and all that that connotes.

Having the freedom of sexual contact with receptive ladies was exhilarating. Those were the days before AIDS came to the forefront, and no one really had the "social disease" fear. I never experienced that type of openness between genders while in the Marine Corps (remember, not only was I married, but that type of social activity was not prominent in the military lifestyle). In The Gallery environment, complimented by the beach attitude of almost "free sex," I found a new area of expression and self-indulgence. To be sure, it was a learning experience. I suppose some guys never outgrow that mode (e.g., fifty-year-old surfers). For me, even just a year of indulgence satisfied me enough to move on. I don't think my personality required constant debauchery, but who knows? Even though I was content to move into a one-person relationship with Candy, and I generally tend to be monogamous anyway, perhaps I could have indulged in that behavior a bit longer. I was still in good shape, was personable, and generally retained an air of attractiveness. I don't know if I would have tired of that lifestyle as I aged, but it might have been interesting to try. Nah....., it was time to move on. The affect of bachelorhood had worn off. Being alone can be a lonely proposition, if you let it. Even in my rapid-fire bachelorhood, I enjoyed my alone time. More so now. Having the time for self-reflection, meditation, or just reading, writing, or TV watching is also necessary for peace of mind and contentment, in most people's lives. My bachelorhood in The Gallery proved that to me, or at least awakened that facet of life in me. I really didn't have much alone time, given the dating and partying. I learned, however, how valuable that can be. When one is constantly on the move, he does not have the time to analyze what's happening in his life. Being an analytical person - left brain predominance in those days, although the development of my right brain skills came to the forefront of my "self" later on - I need that alone time. It one can't be happy with himself alone, it's doubtful he'll be happy surrounded by others.

The overall affect of The Gallery (with its associated bachelorhood, partying, and over-compensation for a former lack of that type of self-indulgence) on my future proved to be "just what the doctor ordered." Timing is everything, as I often exclaim. My entry into that role at age thirty-six was perfect timing for me. I doubt that I , as a slow learner, could have had a more productive bachelorhood at age twenty-three, when I graduated from college. I'll never forget those days. The "group" was wonderfully cohesive, the parties were comprehensively fun, and the availability of "California girls" lived up to its advertising. The scene gave me what I needed it. It was grand!

Chapter 16   Adjusting To Civilian Leadership (Or Lack Thereof)

I feel somewhat qualified to comment on the difference in leadership styles between the military and the corporate worlds. With eleven years as a Marine Corps officer, I am quite familiar with the efficient and effective, although certainly autocratic, manner in which seniors control subordinates. I also have had exposure to various companies in various industries, albeit one field (but with exposure to most fields due to the nature of that single field of corporate security), during my seventeen years in the corporate structure and six years as an outplacement consultant. Furthermore, half of my master's degree had a concentration in Organizational Theory/Behavior/Development.

I may be biased to an extent, primarily because of the cast of characters with whom I interfaced on a regular basis, but I do believe that I am sufficiently competent to discuss how certain individuals to whom I reported (directly or indirectly) in my corporate assignments had an effect - mostly negative - on my tenure in that seventeen-year capacity. I hesitated to include this chapter in this book, which was designed to be upbeat, because I did not really want to address negative issues and detract from the positive theme of the other chapters. However, the presence of the people identified below most definitely affected my on-the-job performance, my attitude and frustration about civilians in general, and my overall development as a person.

In the military, one learns to be obedient. It is the very nature of the demands of the situation. You cannot have a subordinate question your authority in times of combat - it can be a life or death scenario. In combat, there may not be time to hold a conversation in order to examine all sides to an issue. Consequently, the soldier/sailor/airman/Marine is taught unquestioned obedience in boot camp. Once instilled, and believe me what I say it is instilled - more so in some services (e.g., Marine Corps) than others - that obedience is perpetuated ad infinitum in any garrison position. The general public, however, has a misconception of the extent and degree of that obedience flavor. There are times, including in the Marine Corps, when modern management techniques are practiced. An individual, for instance, can be respected for and therefore consulted about his particular expertise, regardless of the respective ranks involved. Proper military decorum is always invoked, but consultations and brainstorming are commonplace, if the situation warrants it. It does create an air of efficiency and effectiveness, while not losing sight of the ingrained need for respect for rank and decision-making responsibility.

There is a significant difference between leadership and management. Many civilians, especially those who have neither a military background nor an education in the principles of those two doctrines, lose sight of that fact. They don't realize that, for example, a person can be a good manager, but a lousy leader. And vice versa. I have witnessed innumerable examples of this truism.

Many books have been written about the Peter Principle. Those elements are almost invariably exhibited by someone who knows nothing of the principles of leadership. Certainly, an individual may not have the education to practice management activities; he is therefore lacking in the tools to do his job. Leadership is something else. Management must be taught, but leadership can be both taught and be a natural ingredient in one's composition. A deficiency in either can lead to an inept "leader" (e.g.., manager), but normally a person in the corporate environment will screw up if he has little conception of the principles of leadership, rather than management.

In my first civilian job as Hughes Aircraft Company (HAC) - I don't count the FBI as being governed by civilian ethos, as any heavily bureaucratic organization has its own structure which can cause degeneration - I reported to one individual (for most of my seven year tenure there), while leaning on another individual at the corporate level for "mentor" advice. In those days, Hughes hired principally ex-FBI agents for its security staff. My direct boss was a real piece of work. We had somewhat of what is described as a "personality clash," but where we differed was in our definition/understanding of that word "leadership." Without getting into too much detail, I'll simply say that, in my opinion, he misperceived the advantage of a military education and therefore hated former military personnel. (Why he hired me in the first place I'll never know, except for the possibility that he put too much stock in me also being ex-Bureau.) He also was devious, inarticulate (I have never seen any Bureau agent or ex-agent with worse interviewing skills), a disruptive interrupter of one-on-one conversation, devoid of innate leadership qualities, a borderline manager of department functions, and such a "kiss-ass" to senior HAC officials and policemen in general that it clouded his responsibilities to his job and his troops. Obviously, I did not enjoy working for this guy. But, give him credit, he mush have had something in his arsenal to allow him twenty-plus years tenure at HAC.

Conversely, there was another individual with whom I originally networked at HAC upon my arrival in Los Angeles, he being the Assistant Director of Corporate Security (a staff rather than line function) and a catalyst for all matters germane to the viability of the pervasive security function throughout all plant sites and ancillary offices. Because he was, I thought (in actuality I later learned he had his own self-serving agenda), open to conversations with people such as me who wanted to learn about the job, he was receptive to being my mentor. I appreciated his concern about my inquiries and well-being, given that I voiced my perspectives about my boss to him (he agreed with my perceptions). In short, my mentor had a positive affect on me learning the business, but unfortunately he disappeared into the "woodwork" when I solicited his help after we had both left the employ of HAC. Because he was frustrated at not being selected for the job of Director of Corporate Security at HAC twice, he eventually moved over to that function (plus other administrative capacities as well, as I understood it) at another aerospace contractor. I truly valued his early assistance, but his lack of response (for whatever reason) to my later networking devalued his overall worthiness as a person, leader, and friend. Perhaps his own agenda superseded his value as a true mentor, which, to me, is a person who never abandons his "student." I did indeed regret his change.

My next job found me at the Corporate Manager of Security (later Director of Corporate Security) for Vidal Sassoon, Inc. I can safely say that this was the best civilian job I ever had. Not only because everyone from Vidal on down respected my expertise in areas which were devoid of attention previously (I was the company's first and only person to fill that role. All positions were eliminated when Vidal decided to sell his company in 1984, four years after my arrival.), but also because both of my reporting seniors - Patrick Gabriele, the VP of Finance, and then Jim Edwards, the VP of Data Processing (I identify both of them, as opposed to others in this chapter, because of their positive influence on me) - were well attuned to doing their jobs with aplomb and creativity. They each had their own idiosyncrasies, but they both were invaluable to me in developing the pervasive security program from scratch. They were both "people persons," and therefore had the respect of all. Their effect on me was of a positive nature, even extending to their whole-hearted support of my avocational activities with the American Society for Industrial Security (ASIS). Thank you, gentlemen; I wish you well in whatever endeavors you pursue.

The remainder of my corporate security career was disastrous. Unfortunately, I could not advance that career by doing what I did best, namely the development of security programs for a firm which had none. Timing is everything, as I've said before. I could not afford to wait for that right opportunity, so I joined General Dynamics in San Diego as an assistant to the Convair Division security manager. He was a recently retired USAF bird colonel who had no industrial security background, had somehow snowed his boss (the VP of Industrial Relations, who had a similar abrasive personality), and had created such hate-and discontent within our organization that I was obliged to be the scapegoat in an organizational shake-up a year and a half later. His name is not important, his nickname (as applied by my troops) was "The Giant White Slug," and his propensity was to "cover his own ass," regardless of the truth and consequences of the matter at hand. Here was a senior military man who had obviously never learned about modern management techniques or how to lead people toward the accomplishment of the mission and the welfare of his people. He proved to be a real pathetic iconoclast.

Following the General Dynamics fiasco, I moved to San Jose in order to help out my friend Jim Royer (see Chapter 23). He was the Corporate Director of Security for FMC, a multi-organizational conglomerate in Chicago. Their division in San Jose had a young Security Manager whom I had met at an ASIS function, who needed some help from someone like me who had a more comprehensive understanding of the needs of the security program. Although I envisioned a good working relationship with that individual, he apparently viewed me as a threat to his job and authority. I admit to having had my own personal problems at the time (see Chapter 21 on Dona Stevenson), which may have clouded my thought processes at times, but I tried not to let it affect my performance on the job. Eventually, he used my vulnerability to create a chasm between us, instead of trying to support me in my personal dilemma. That chasm widened to the extent that senior management recognized it.

When the incumbent Security Manager left FMC for another position, I was not selected to replace him, even though I was by far the most qualified candidate. Instead, another young and inexperienced person was brought in from another division, primarily, as I understand it from Jim Royer, because his job was eliminated in that city and management wanted to retain him for future potential. Even in my disappointment, I vowed to support him, and did all I could, even after he disregarded my comprehensive value during a departmental reorganization. Again to keep it brief, that clown affected my overall perspective of a "diminished capacity" civilian demeanor by doing the opposite of what is supposed to be measures to incorporate modern management techniques and the application of effective principles of leadership. By now, I was getting more and more disillusioned with the corporate world.

It took me two more ventures into corporate security before I finally made the career change into outplacement services. I guess I'm a slow learner! Anyway, returning to Southern California after two years in San Jose, I took a position in retail security, in which I had an interest, with a major discount retailer. Its corporate security director was a former Marine whom I had briefly known during my active days in ASIS. That organization was experiencing growing pains. He had been with them from day one. But running a "mom-and-pop" outfit is considerably different from establishing a comprehensive security/loss prevention program. He recognized my experience in that mode and brought me in to get things administratively squared away. What I didn't know about him was that he was a total and unbending autocrat. It affected our working relationship. I left the Marine Corps as a Major; he was an enlisted man who never made it beyond the rank of corporal. I think he liked this role reversal. After several inordinate and inappropriate attempts by him to evoke "obedience" from me, regardless of the actual circumstances of the program development, I finally had to inform him of "who was who, and what was what." It alleviated the tension temporarily. I could see, however, that he was not going to change. Shortly thereafter, the company was the victim of a hostile take-over. When senior management eliminated forty percent of middle management positions to show the shareholders how efficient they were (In actuality, that was a ridiculous endeavor.), I welcomed egress from that environment. With senior management, which paid its president nearly a million dollars in base compensation alone, chopping middle management to "save money" (but really to protect their - senior management - jobs), I knew I had finally had it with this corporate environment.

In 1990, I made my career change into outplacement services. About a year later, I compromised myself by accepting a position I couldn't refuse, back in corporate security. A manufacturer and distributor of sports oriented trading cards had a need for someone to upgrade their security program, or so they said. I accepted the position because of the challenge and the money. I thought that I would be able to effectively work with my new boss, another young fellow who held the title of VP of operations. We had a mutual military background, he being a former West Point Army man. What I didn't see during the interviewing process, however, was his volatile personality, his unyielding propensity for doing it his way, his inability to handle pressure (by tossing a baseball in the air, much like Captain Queeg of the Caine Mutiny did with the ball bearings rolling in his hand, during any kind of conversation, one-on-one or staff meeting), and his (as well as his boss' - the president) unjustified paranoia about theft. The conflict that arose between us was mutually unbearable, so I returned to the outplacement field.

I incorporate this chapter into my book because I think it illustrates that I was not a happy camper in my roles within the corporate security environment. I'm sure my attitude and behavior had a bearing on a few of the situations at hand, but I am convinced that my dichotomous relationship with my reporting seniors - those with a military background and those without - was based on a combination of my never having "let go" of my preference for the military and their lack of understanding of the principles of leadership. Perhaps I had an unilateral perspective, but I don't regard myself as stubborn. There are times when change is needed. When I could not impress my values upon others, I may have become malcontent, difficult to work with, and biased.

Nevertheless, my perspective that my civilian seniors negatively affected my career still holds water for me. I don't think that is being a professional malcontent. Their shortcomings affected my demeanor, I suppose, and that led to many years of frustration.

Chapter 17 Christine: My "Drinking Buddy"

Drinking buddies are hard to find. Anyone can have a drink with anyone else at any locale. It takes a special bond between two people to be "drinking buddies," however. At least in my vernacular.

Christine married a gunnery sergeant in my command at Camp Pendleton soon after I assumed the reins as Officer-in-Charge of the airfield at Camp Pendleton in 1968. It appeared to be a good match. Although I didn't know Charlie that well initially (he was my electronics SNCO - Staff Non-Commissioned Officer), and I certainly didn't know Chris, they were rapidly to become the social phenomenon for my outfit. She owned (from a former marriage) a rambling ranch type home on a mountain top in Escondido. With its massive pool and deck area, it was an ideal site for a party. And there were a few. Although the military decorum was maintained when I socialized with my troops, even when everyone was "under the influence," the mixture of her Scottish and English friends (Chris was born in Scotland and could pour on the brogue) with my troops made for a nice blend for a lively party. There are innumerable stories that could be told, but for illustration purposes to set the "drinking buddy" scene, I mention just a few.

My first tid-bit actually occurred at my home in Carlsbad rather than at their mountain top retreat. I believe it was soon after their wedding that I held the mandatory (by Marine Corps etiquette) organizational social function for my officers and SNCOs, a total of about twenty personnel (including wives). I also had a couple of officer friends from other organizations over. Predominate in that latter was Jack Palmer (whom I had originally met at the Development Center in Quantico - he was General Walt's aid-de-camp - in the mid-sixties) and his soon-to-be bride Jean (who is my daughter Michelle Jean's namesake -middle name obviously - they being her godparents). I mention them because of a subsequent story.

The formal aspect of my social function served its purpose. However, as Marines will tend to do, the guys gravitated to one part of my house to exchange war stories, while the distaff side of the group were left to fend for themselves. Well, the discussion of recipes, babies, and other female related subjects was not to the liking of Christine. Feigning a headache, she finally convinced Charlie that they should be the first to leave. As they were departing, Christine said words to the effect of "Thank you for a wonderful time, Mr. Anderson." Mostly with "tongue in cheek" humor, but with an educational thrust toward this new Marine wife, I responded by saying "That's Major Anderson, not Mister." (Note: For military bearing purposes, let me inform the reader that the Marine Corps does not use the term "Mister" for addressing an officer, as does the Navy.) Although she held her contempt in for Charlie's sake, Christine was to later unleash to her husband her perspective of my arrogant "straight-laced" rigidity. No harm, no foul, however. Throughout my civilian years, we both regarded this introductory stiffness with hilarity, especially given our friendship and future very informal and expletive greetings which match the terms of endearment of two French Foreign Legionnaires at times.

As mentioned, I experienced many grand times at social gatherings at their hacienda with a view of the whole world. Without too much elaboration, let me just list a few epics that come to mind.

- [ ] The aforementioned Jack Palmer, whose driving skills were impaired by a few rum-and-cokes, departing a party by driving his VW bug over the hill - backwards - with only the cascading shrubbery preventing him from going all the way down the mountain and he becoming a statistic.

- [ ] A couple of my former troops (I was a civilian by then) holding the bathroom door knob to prevent me from exiting the "head," while their cohorts (and Christine's ten-twelve-year old son) took snapshots of my voluptuous and bra-less Candy for future dissemination. For some time thereafter, I thought there was a malfunction of the door!

- [ ] My either losing my balance or intentionally doing a "carr-qual" (carrier qualification landing) - who remembers?! - onto a couple of nearby occupied tables from my original position on the diving board. Some impression to make on Chris' civilian friends by an "officer and gentleman."

- [ ] My showing up at one of their parties (vintage '73-'74) with a date (Loralie, whose sister Sheila I also dated) who wore a pendant around her neck in the form of male genitals. My former young troops (as well as other attendees) relished initiating conversations with her.

- [ ] My Marine Corps farewell party at their home, which proved to be raucous, highly informal now that my troops could call me "Ed" instead of "Major," and sentimental (given my extreme reluctance to leave the Corps and this command - see Chapter 12).

I did not maintain much contact with Chris or Charlie during the next few years. My adventures in the Pacific Northwest with the FBI and Los Angeles in my new civilian career allowed for only occasional follow-up to the "good ol' days." I guess it was about ten years or so after I departed Camp Pendleton that I learned about their divorce. It was then that Chris and I started to mutually share our heartbreaks and misgivings, most especially after Dona and I split. Christine had met virtually every woman I had ever dated or married. She could therefore cast her judgments about my activities rather poignantly. In fact, she never pulled any punches in her evaluations, sometimes much to my chagrin! Of them all, however, I believe that Chris had most fond memories of the relationship Dona and I had. In fact, they're still quasi-friends, as much as distance separation will permit (Chris doesn't like to travel much these days, even up to Orange County).

Christine's affect on me has been enormous. She has provided a safe haven for me a couple of times when I found myself homeless after a divorce/separation. She has given a very soft and understanding shoulder for me to figuratively cry on during my discussions of my love life. She has continually opened her home and bar to me to interact with her friends and at times with some of my former troops. And she has always "been there" for me in any situation in which I needed conversation, solace, and/or understanding. As it would be with friends, the reciprocity has also been present. I believe that I have provided a stability and friendship - in all its forms - for her during her trials and tribulations. We have had our own respective circle of friends and acquaintances (e.g., her fellow countrymen from Scotland and my bachelorhood cronies - see Chapter 15), but I think we are both better people for having had each other as drinking buddies for a goodly number of years, sporadic or not. People are still amazed when we assure them that our relationship is strictly platonic, given our otherwise closeness.

Christine is a unique individual and a loyal friend. She speaks her mind and we have different perspectives on certain matters. But there has been no one who better deserves the title of "friend" than she for me through the years, except for my too short of a relationship with Dona, who was not only my mate/lover/companion, but my all-time best friend as well. Nevertheless, Chris, you have stood as a lighthouse for me during some dire times. I love you, buddy, for all you have done for me, in good times as well as not-so-good. Semper Fi!

As a postscript to this chapter, I had considered not elaborating on Chris' effect on me, primarily because of her request for privacy. I decided to not honor her request, however, as this chapter was originally designed to be one of my most altruistic, with a focus on a person whom I deemed to be my best friend for the longest period of time. These words were also to illustrate quite succinctly and poignantly how a man and a woman can become very close friends without having the complications of a romantic or sexual relationship. That in itself is important. Using my best judgment, I have decided to invoke my First Amendment rights, overriding her request for anonymity. Any book about my life without mention of Christine's presence would be an oversight of incalculable proportions.

Chapter 18 Dudley and Covelle Jude

They are long-time friends, she more than he, time wise. The purpose of including this chapter in my book is primarily two-fold. I'll address the issue of male-female friendship, as I did in the previous chapter, and I want to relate an anecdotal event about my introduction to Dudley, notably it being a revelation to me about acquired or innate tolerance toward a different perspective on a major issue, and how that meeting awakened my theretofore unilateral thoughts about the country-splitting Viet Nam issue.

Covelle and I first met in 1973 when I took my first civilian job at Hughes Aircraft Company in Los Angeles. As a secretary to an assets procurement and materials control manager (for lack of a more accurate title), her office was only a few doors away from mine in the Personnel Security Department. It was inevitable that we should meet, she being an attractive and bubbly blond, and me having my new bachelor antennas out already. We dated for a while, discovered that our interests varied at the moment, and then became very close friends. I mentioned in another chapter that I thought it strange that I, who had been almost totally oriented to male friendships in my Marine Corps days, became heavily focused toward female relationships almost as soon as I became a civilian. There is no logical explanation for that metamorphosis, except that environment was probably the principal factor. The salient aspect of the transformation was that I now found females more interesting than males. How that happened is an unknown. At that time of my life (1973+), I had not yet become fully cognizant (not that I am today) of the "Men Are From Mars; Women Are From Venus" theme. Somehow, however, I found women to be intriguing, not so much from the dating perspective, but from their dichotomous approaches, attitudes, and actions when compared to their male counterparts. It was refreshing and enlightening to openly discuss both trivial and important issues with some of the women I encountered.

I also previously mentioned that it is difficult for me to acquire a true friend, male or female, because of my propensity for background commonality (e.g., military; aviation; sports). During my Bachelorhood at The Gallery (see Chapter 15), and to this very day, I've preferred the company of females, without any undertones of sexual conquest. There were several males of diverse ages and backgrounds in our "group" at The Gallery, and I thoroughly enjoyed the camaraderie we established in the partying vein. I do not recall, however, having too many, if any, serious conversations with the guys. Not so with the female participants. I found many of them, as I do today in my casual contacts, receptive to more than locker room or bar room "sea stories" of inconsequential substance. Granted, no one is more open to knocking down a few cold ones while "solving the world's problems" with the guys than I am. And some serious conversations have developed during those times, to varying degrees. But women have a different outlook on many matters, and I enjoy hearing about and discussing them. I suppose one could translate that chit-chat as my having a "gossip" nature, but conversely I have found the male-female conversation more engrossing and romantically picturesque, if not dynamic.

My perpetuating friendship with Covelle (as with others mentioned above) is based on mutual respect, sincere liking of our individual personas, appreciation for laughter, an understanding of

61

the fine line between humorous sarcasm and hurtful criticism, a concern for our buddy's well-being, and all the other tender couplings that are the rudimentary elements for being a friend. We have helped each other on occasion during the transitions of our respective marital difficulties. She even linked me to her best friend in Sacramento a few years back, it proving to be a wonderful, albeit short, encounter. Why it was such a short relationship with Barbara is another matter, the sad story of which will not be addressed herein.

A few years back (ten plus or minus), Covelle semi-prepared me for an introduction to her new love-life, namely Dudley Jude. She had been seeing him for a while and had arrived at the conclusion that this was "Mr. Right." Now in her early forties, with lost opportunities in previous marriages, she intended to match Elizabeth Taylor's marital record (not really, but the humorous thought prevails here). Like Liz every time, she was convinced that Dud was her lucky charm for longevity (I'm being facetious about the analogy; Covelle and Dud have now passed their ninth year of marital bliss and are still going strong). In fact, the ultimate sign that this match is for life is the presence of their son Jason, who was conceived on their honeymoon. That in itself is a story and a half, since Covelle was childless to that point, had a belief that she could not conceive, and therefore did not use any birth control device/method in any of her marriages. On this honeymoon, however, Jason cried out to his forty-one-year-old potential mama that he wanted to see daylight in nine months. Jason was a glorious and welcomed addition to what I perceive to be an enviable relationship.

Anyway, back to my introduction to Dudley. Covelle told me she was hesitant to introduce us, but wouldn't be specific. The actual meeting went according to the norm; I couldn't understand her apprehension. As we were talking backgrounds, my Marine Corps tenure came up. Without an apologetic or shameful note, Dud said he spent his military associated years dodging Uncle Sam. Given that I had pursued some of those individuals while in the FBI, I inquired about that matter further. I did not notice Covelle cringing off to the side.

Here's the rub. Dudley was a draft-dodger! He was your typical long-haired anti-war activist who burned his draft card and fled prosecution. Knowing that I was proud of my Marine Corps association, Covelle figured that I would respond in some negative fashion to Dud's revelation. Not so. Yes, I was and still am a gung-ho Marine at heart. But even after a few years of friendship, Covelle didn't realize, and perhaps I didn't either, that my tolerance for a different perspective about that war was a part of me. I thought we had sufficiently discussed my thoughts and disillusionment about that political war. Maybe we did; maybe my overall pride and esprit-de-corps clouded her judgment as to my reaction to his non-military activities. She wanted to retain our friendship, and she wanted Dud and me to become friends also. But she was one up-tight broad that introductory evening until Dud broke the ice. My response was essentially "It ain't no big deal." She was concurrently amazed and relieved.

I think my acceptance of Dud's anti-military stance affected me more than it did Covelle, and that's saying something. Perhaps neither of us expected me to be understanding of his resistance to the draft. By that time, I no longer wore the uniform I so cherished, and therefore no longer

Author's longtime friends
Dudley and Covelle Jude, with their son, Jason.

had my "horse-blinders" on concerning the polarization that existed in the sixties and seventies. I did my job while I wore the uniform; I'm quite sure I projected the typical military perspectives and slogans while an active duty "jar-head."

My reversal of attitude and my acceptance of Dud's integrity did not mean that I had lost my attachment to the principles of the Marine Corps. As far as I'm concerned, "Once A Marine, Always A Marine." That is part of what "Semper Fidelis" means to a former Marine. By the time I had met Dudley, I had changed in many ways. His draft-dodging flight didn't threaten me, nor did it nauseate me. That introductory night was a revelation to all four of us (Dona - see Chapter 21 - was there too), in a very positive manner. Whereas Covelle had been a long standing friend, Covelle and Dudley are now long-standing friends. The introduction of the draft-dodger to the consummate Marine turned out to be just another good story to whip out during a party. It is also a story that binds.

Chapter 19 Sue Dickinson: My Roomie

This Chapter completes the trilogy of my female friends who have had the greatest impact on the value I attach to this category. Sue Dickinson ranks up there with Christine and Covelle for her own unique reasons. Like Covelle, I met her as soon as I started my bachelorhood, she being a resident of The Gallery (see Chapter 15). Sue was to become an integral part of "the group," and more importantly grew in stature from a casual partier to a close confidant, despite her moving to Las Vegas sixteen-seventeen years ago to pursue a more rewarding life style with her new-born son.

I have a terrible memory, so I don't specifically remember the circumstances of our first meeting. It could have been at the pool/spa when Wayne Bradshaw initially took me by hand for introductory purposes. Or we may have stumbled onto each other in the hallways of The Gallery, Sue occupying the apartment directly adjacent to mine. It was probably an instantaneous liking, given that we're both from the New York City area, she from Long Island and I from Westchester County. Sue was also a flight attendant for a private charter airline, so our common interest in aviation may have caused a catalytic coupling.

Sue Dickinson at the helm, with
Jeff and Michelle at the lower left.

As I mentioned in Chapter 15, our "group" participated in numerous social activities. Both Sue and I were in the middle of the festivities on virtually every occasion. That in itself was enough to form a bonding. Little did we know, however, that our friendship was to blossom far beyond my liaisons with "the group." Most of those people have gone on to their own independent ventures, whereas Sue and I maintained contact.

As I have done in other chapters, perhaps I can highlight some of my recollections of my early interactions with Sue in a "bullet" fashion.

☐ A Cinco de Mayo celebration in The Gallery in which we all contributed a specialty dish for a brunch in the recreation room. Amazingly, I remember my contribution to that mass of delectables - a few trays of egg burritos - but I cannot recall Sue's. Whatever it was, it must have been a highlight, for she was a consummate cook, especially for group gatherings. The brunch was a huge success and led to several other similar functions within the walls of that beach fraternity/sorority.

☐ The Renaissance Faire in Los Angeles (initially in the hills of Agoura; now in the flatlands of a suburb of Riverside) is a marvelous setting for a party. I didn't miss that annual affair for ten straight years, but I'll never forget the first one that our group attended. I believe Sue was the instigator. Regardless, I remember my semi-partnership with her that day (I didn't have a date), in which we shared wine-filled bota bags, "dinosaur" ribs, and sausage-and-onion "bangers" as we strolled through the side shows and avenues of that delightful fun-filled excursion into the villages of Queen Elizabeth I. Sue's constant smile and insatiable appetite for the good times set the tone for the day, as seen in the attached photo of Sue and "Igor," as we named him.

Sue Dickinson with cast member at Renaissance Faire

☐ My birthday - October 11 - became a ritual for Sue. By that time (seven months into my residence at The Gallery), we had established a strong friendship, again without need for boy-girl physical contact. Even during subsequent years, Sue would invite several people to her place to celebrate my B-day. The first was unique, in that my left foot was in a cast up to my knee from having torn my Archilles tendon. One of her B-day gifts to me was a T-shirt bearing the inscription "The Gallery's Own Champion Sprinter." (See photo depicting this Gallery highlight.)

Sue Dickinson (standing) hosting author's birthday party at The Gallery,
with appropriate commemorative T-shirt (note the cast on leg).

☐ During the Christmas-New Year holiday week of 1973, we originated a frolicking
retreat up to Lake Arrowhead. I believe that Sue was again one of the "founding
fathers." That encampment for a week proved to be one of the highlights of the
year for "the group." The first trek was specifically memorable because of an
announcement that Sue made the day before we left. I made mention in Chapter
fifteen that, as a rule-of-thumb, no one in the group actually dated a co-member of
that group. Sue was the first to break that rule with her announcement that she
and a Galleryite nicknamed "Fireman Bill" would be sleeping together at the house
we rented in Arrowhead. The announcement stunned us all. Maybe not so much
because it violated an unwritten law, but probably because of the people involved.
It didn't seem like a good match to most of us (in the long run it wasn't).
Nevertheless, it did not hamper the outstanding party scene in the mountainous
snow and luxury "cabin."

☐ I guess I shouldn't be critical of Sue's attachment to Bill. It was a similar
situation with me and Candy. Sue, bless her little heart, could never understand
why Candy and I were a couple, given our basic differences. The astonishment of
our coupling was realized in early March 1975 when another couple announced
their engagement and wedding date. Candy always liked attention in her then
hedonistic way. As a means of upstaging our friends' engagement proclamation,
Candy bellowed out that we had been secretly married a few days before. Of all
the perfunctory congratulations we received, Sue was the most straight-forward in
proclaiming her concern to me privately that the match was not a good one. She
was right, as the next paragraph explains.

Two months after our wedding (Covelle and her then husband Jim stood up for us in a private garden/gazebo ceremony), Candy and I had another one of our disagreements. We therefore separated. Again, timing is everything. Concurrent to our separation, Sue was in the process of relocating her residence. So we put our heads together and decided to be roommates. Hence, I forever attached the nickname "Roomie" to Sue. The actual live-in didn't last long, but the affectionate connotation has stuck.

The Gallery group pitched in to help us move our respective belongings into our new apartment in Hermosa Beach (unfortunately, nothing was available at The Gallery). I wasn't much help, still being in my cast from the surgery on my Archilles tendon. For the next two months, Sue and I had an ideal roommate relationship, not getting in either of our ways. She was even reluctantly cooperative in allowing Candy on the premises during our exploration of reconciliation. Well, that term became a fact a scant two months after we moved in. As I hobbled up the staircase on my crutches one evening, I found Candy waiting for me with a baby doll in hand. With her revelation that she was pregnant, we decided to give the relationship another shot. I hated leaving Sue high-and-dry, but she proved to be an understanding friend - again - in wishing us well.

The next major event of my cohesive bonding with Sue occurred a couple of years later. Sue's biological clock was ticking. At the time, she was not fully involved with anyone, although there were always a couple of guys on the periphery. A monumental decision was made by her when she announced to those of us who were close to her that she was going to search for an ideal person who would father a child. Sue sincerely wanted to have a baby out of wedlock, with no strings attached (e.g., monetary child support from the father). She found her mate and conceived. Her plan was to do a natural child birth at home, using a professional mid-wife and a couple of friends to help in the delivery. Naturally, I volunteered to assist, having gone through the Lamaze method with Candy in giving birth to Misty. Probably more out of convention than an intentional slight to me, Sue chose a couple of female friends to be present at that event. I was disappointed, but I understood. All went well, with little Ronnie being born on Halloween.

I couldn't even become much of a visiting "godparent," as Sue decided to abandon the Southern California lifestyle in order to raise Ronnie in an environment more conducive to child-rearing. She decided on Las Vegas, and has been there since in her new vocation of - guess what - a game dealer in the casinos, although at one juncture she returned to the airline industry in order to be the Director of In-Flight Attendants (for lack of her formal title). It didn't last long, as that start-up organization folded from a lack of business.

Since her relocation to Las Vegas, I have had occasion to visit with her several times, including a two month stay following my divorce from K.C. in 1992 while I networked with senior security management personnel in the casinos, my viewing a possible relocation to that tinsel town (it didn't happen). Sue was more than hospitable each time. What could one expect from a long standing friend? No strings and no hassles. She was, and still is, a peach of a gal. I have been blessed with the friendship of diverse people who have made my existence a happy one. I am a great believer in friendship; there have been times where I have said truthfully that I hold friendship in higher value than intimate relationships. There are certainly advantages to each. The glory of a coupling of friendship with a romance, as I had with Dona, is the supreme measure of happiness. Short of a romance by standard definition - I think friendship has a certain romanticism to it, regardless of gender - my involvement with such wonderful, giving, and caring females as Christine, Covelle, and Sue has made my transition through the civilian years a helluva lot more bearable.

Chapter 20   The Birth Of My Daughter Misty Dawn

Following the inevitable breakup of my relationship with Suzanne Pedersen in Portland, my resignation from the FBI, and my separation from my wife Pat, I chose to seek out new horizons in Southern California, the site of my geographic preference because of the weather, life style, and fond memories from my Marine Corps days in Orange County and the Camp Pendleton/San Diego area. As a native New Yorker who embraced everything about Southern California, I knew my destiny was on the beaches (or at least nearby - but certainly not Barstow or Needles!) of sunny Southern California.

My tall #2 bride, Candy.

As I mentioned, my first priority (well actually my second, if you count getting a job as number one) was getting myself squared away concerning the learning curve on relationships and "What's it all about, Alfie?" As soon as I networked and began my new career in corporate security management at Hughes Aircraft Company in Los Angeles, I took an apartment on the beach and sought out a therapist. The individual I chose had a great effect on me and my development, but I'm not making that experience a separate chapter - too heavy, and I'm probably not qualified to write comprehensively about all of the aspects of self-enlightenment and self-actualization.

The next thing I did was violate the cardinal rule against the edict of: "Never get involved/married too quickly after a divorce." Actually, I did enjoy a productive and lively bachelorhood in Hermosa Beach for about a year before I compromised myself. I did everything I set out to do. I learned from therapy, I dated a variety of women without total involvement, and I played the partying role. But, alas, one never knows when cupid will strike again. From all the books I read during my therapy, I shouldn't have gotten involved with someone for about a year and a half, preferably two. I was adhering to that premise, and then Candy Michelle Mitchell entered my life.

Candy was my physical ideal. A six foot blond built like the proverbial "brick s--- house" (bad analogy, as her face and body more approximated a goddess than an outhouse). She had just turned twenty-two (I was thirty-eight). I was warned about "robbing the cradle" and that we were not a good match, despite the partying theme we were both operating under. But I was blinded by her beauty and my fantasy of having a much younger beauty be attracted to me. I eventually recognized that we had different value systems, primarily based on our age/experience levels. Nevertheless, we dated, became emotionally involved (despite our almost constant bickering), moved in together, and then married less than a year after our meeting. When we broke the news to our friends (our wedding wasn't an elopement; we just had one couple act as state-required witnesses), most were gracious in offering congratulations. But one or two voiced concern. They were right. Two months after the wedding, we separated (one of several during our dating sequence). Two months later she showed up on my doorstep with a baby doll in hand. Yes, the rabbit bit the dust. I guess our reuniting was a forced affair because of her pregnancy, but we tried to make the best of it, including taking the Lamaze birthing method lessons together. I think the pregnancy and Lamaze brought us closer together, at least on the surface. We still had personality and value clashes. And then the day arrived - December 25, 1975.

The event of Misty Dawn's birth was undoubtedly the single-most exciting, exhilarating, impressive, significant, and blessed event of my life. I have already related how positively the adoption of my other two children affected me, but this was different. I have never - and still don't - differentiated between my kids being adopted or natural born entries into my life. I love all three of them equally. The actual birthing - meaning I assisted in and observed the birth of Misty - was an amazing feat. Candy and I had religiously practiced the Lamaze technique, and then we both worked our proverbial butts off during the labor, with Candy experiencing the delivery pain - although her concentration during the process was exemplary in controlling the pain - while I busted my back providing massage and encouragement.

Here it comes!!! She was still an "it," since we chose not to learn of the baby's sex beforehand. First the crown of the head. Then the torso in a rather precarious manner. Fortunately, no delivery complications, although the forceps threat lured as a possibility. And finally her legs. I literally shouted "It's a Misty Dawn!" when I determined in my infinite wisdom the gender of the baby. I beamed with enormous pride. I could hardly believe what I had just witnessed. We had viewed births on screen during the Lamaze sessions, but there's nothing like first-hand experience. I kissed Candy in a sincere demonstration of love, thankfulness, and, as I said, enormous pride (of course, fathers are solely responsible for the production process; the mother is only the delivery tool! I'm only kidding, Candy!).

I believe it was only a seven-hour labor; not bad for a first-born. Everything went well. Candy handled the natural child birth without too much trouble, never once calling for Demerol. Her not taking pain-killing drugs amazed me, having remembered the comedienne Carol Burnett's proclamation that giving birth was like pulling your lower lip up over your head. I never really understood that metaphor, but I appreciated the inference of pain. I've had my share of pain, particularly from sprained ankles in basketball, which literally ended my playing days while in the Marine Corps. I also held up well while providing support to Candy during the labor, a la the Lamaze method.

71

Brand new Misty Dawn with her proud parents.

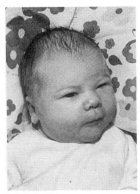

No Winston Churchill here; Misty definitely resembles my mother at birth.

Misty's first Christmas and birthday (December 26, 1976) with author and Candy looking on.

Author with Candy (wife #2) at Los Angeles Playboy Club (circa 1974)

And now, I was a father again, this time having gone through the ecstasy of participating in the actual birth.

What an amazing and satisfying event. Despite our problems, I truly loved Candy. And now we were a family, which I hoped would solidify our marriage (a typical misconception by people

73

having marital problems and not seeking professional help). I even looked forward to raising Misty myself much of the time - Candy was a flight attendant and on the road a lot. And I was certainly excited about both my parents and my other kids sharing in the wonderment of Misty coming into the Anderson family. They say all babies initially look like Winston Churchill. Not Misty Dawn, whose name Candy suggested as a derivative from an advertisement for a soap (I believe) named Misty Morn (a bit corny, but nevertheless a very pretty name for a very pretty girl). She was a facial replica of my mother. Misty could never have been misidentified in a hospital nursery mix-up; I would have recognized her immediately. I do remember saying "poor kid," referring to her resemblance to my side of the family. I wished she looked more like Candy. that beauty streak being more to my liking (Misty today at age twenty still bears my features - poor kid - but she has certain facial and mannerism characteristics that parallel her mother).

Misty Dawn, you were truly an amazement. Your birth - the actual event itself and the symbolism of life and family perpetuation that it represented - was and is the apex of my existence. I have never felt such love, joy, exhilaration, pride, comfort, satisfaction, unbounded happiness, passion for life, expectations for the future, and relief that you were physically sound (that has always been a concern of mine) as when I watched you being born. It is almost an indescribable experience. Again, not to take anything away from the witnessing of the adoptions of Jeff and Michelle, but I suppose witnessing the birth of your first-born by natural means has a special place in every parent's heart. That day was some kind of a belated Christmas gift!

The cake reflects the kid's joint zodiac sign, all Capricorns

10-year-old Misty practicing on a surfboard in our Tustin home pool. She does it for real now!

Author with Misty at Christmas time, 1991.

Your life, Misty Dawn, has been nothing but sheer pleasure for me. I wish I could be with you forever, for I know that you will be as wonderful an adult as you were a baby, child, adolescent, and young lady. Thanks, sweetie. You have indeed affected me to the max!

As a postscript, I also want to say , "Thank You," to Candy, not only for producing such a bundle of joy, but for raising her (even in the remoteness of Alaska) from age one through sixteen in such an exemplary manner. Misty came back home to Southern California, much to her preference, to live with me at that age. Candy, you done good, babe! I'm sorry we couldn't have done it together.

Author with daughter, Misty, 1994

Chapter 21 Dona: The "Love Of My Life"

When my number two wife (Candy) and I divorced - with Candy taking my daughter Misty to live in Alaska in early 1977 (just after her first birthday) - I typically thought that I would never be able to love again, at least not to the extent that I had just experienced. I had lost my physical ideal (or so I thought until I met Dona), my natural-born-one-year-old, and the comforting feeling of a family, especially since my eleven-year-old son Jeff was en route from his mother in Colorado to live with me. Another destabilizing and mind-boggling trauma for me to deal with! How many of these things did I have to go through before I hit the right one? Are multiple heartbreaks the norm? What can I do to recover and "let go?"

Call me "lucky." I have always bounced back from life's little foibles rather nicely. This transition proved no different. But they all require time, that great healer.

Ed and Dona during happier moments

Soon after Candy and Misty departed the scene - and a year before I met this chapter's titlist - I met a provocative (a la Suzanne from Chapter 13) young lady named Shelly, who also worked at Hughes Aircraft Company, but at another facility in the vast Los Angeles complex of that major employer (ninety thousand people world-wide at that time). I didn't know it, of course, but Shelly would prove to be an excellent transition for me from one major player in my life to the next.

Author with Dona and children, Misty, Michelle and Jeff at Tustin, CA home. (circa early 1980s)

Shelly loved to make love, and I loved that. My romantic activities with Candy had been almost nil for some time for several reasons. So Shelly was a welcomed addition to my life style. One complication, however, was that my son had just moved in with me, and I suspect I neglected him in favor of again pursuing romance. I wanted to teach Jeff independence, but I may have gone too far. I'm not sure whether Jeff suffered from being on his own at that age. His possible perspective that another female was the root cause of his being "abandoned" again (Remember, he knew he was adopted and he harbored strong resentment toward his mother, Pat, because of her "tough love" applications following our divorce.) may have triggered his reaction to Dona and me becoming a couple a year henceforth. I'll address that a bit more in subsequent paragraphs.

Shelly and I lasted about a year. We had fun and romance, but apparently I had not yet "let go" of Candy. It showed. As a matter of fact, I stated same to her in a rather abrupt manner toward the end of that year. Not too smart. So we split. I guess her evaluation of me was true, that I was the most inconsiderate considerate person she had ever met.

One day later I met Dona (again, I delete her surname for discretion's sake). She was to become the source of the best relationship I have ever had, problems notwithstanding.

Dona also worked for Hughes, which had a recreational facility in El Segundo (Dona's home territory) with a backyard that housed a volleyball court. A number of us had established an informal weekday game with rotating players, informal meaning "jungle" rules and beer drinking. What the hell, it was good exercise while still fitting the partying theme I enjoyed and practiced as often as possible.

It was an inauspicious meeting. And yet, something drew me to Dona. I intuitively knew, I think, that our next meeting would develop into at least a "date." Probably more.

One week after our initial introduction, I asked Dona if she wanted to go on a "beer run" with me (the game had unforgivably been depleted of that vital sustenance!). She replied in the affirmative, we talked for a bit during that beverage acquisition, and we continued the liaison after the conclusion of the games.

I was never so at ease with a woman as I was with Dona. I was naturally attracted to her long blond hair, athletic body of perfect proportions, and vivacious spirit. I also recognized that I genuinely liked this person. I didn't necessarily see her only as a potential physical conquest: I really wanted to know her better. Although we quickly consummated a romantic involvement (I won't reveal the details, but it was unique - she always spoke fondly of the sweat - and we both have reflected back on that initiation with mutual smiles), the evolution of this relationship into an investigation of permanence became the crux of this involvement.

We discovered that our interests were synonymous and we enjoyed each other's company. I think the relationship was based on our ability to have fun together. There wasn't anything that we didn't mutually like, be it our internal personalities or external activities. Our passion and compassion grew, our perspectives about important issues were generally in consonance, and we

Happier days at our Tustin home:
Ed, Dona, and Jeff, with Sunshine and Muffin

accepted our individual frailties, idiosyncrasies, and intellectual variances as ingredients which made the relationship interesting. We even had "our" song - Billy Joel's "I Love You Just The Way You Are." That proved not to be accurate, however. But the continuous coupling of romanticism was further enhanced musically - and more poignantly - by Neil Diamond's "Hello, Again, Hello" and Barry Manilow's "Somewhere Down The Road."

There were differences, to be sure, and they unfortunately became the basis for our eventual demise nine years later. It is sad but true; if a couple doesn't wholeheartedly work on communications and understanding, the differences will overcome the similarities. More on that later.

Dona and I moved in together somewhat over a year after we met. That commitment was preceded by our engagement, which was a scene in itself. Christmas Eve 1978 at her father's house in El Segundo, I presented her with a huge box wrapped in Christmas paper. Tearing it apart, she could find nothing in the box full of crumpled newspaper. I told her to be more thorough in her search. In one corner of the over-sized container she located a standard size box that usually contains a ring. It did. I had previously learned that Dona did not care for diamonds. So....., she opened the smaller box to find a rather exquisite jade (her favorite stone) ring. I immediately got on my knees, in full view of her father, and proposed marriage. I wish I could remember the words I used; they did the job. With exuberance she accepted, her father nodded approval, and I flushed with happiness. It was a grand highlight of our almost six month courtship.

Living together posed an almost immediate problem. My son Jeff, now thirteen, had already exhibited signs of maladjustments, particularly store shoplifting and truancy from school. And here was another threat - in his psyche, as I subsequently learned - to stability in his life. I wrote his behavior off to typical teenage growing pains, but it was apparently deeper than that. Dona began to have some of her possessions disappear. Nothing of significant monetary value, but nevertheless an irritant to her. We eventually found a couple of those items (e.g., records) hidden in the house. Obviously, Jeff was the prime suspect. As was his nature, he denied any culpability. The continuation of these little (major to Dona) anomalies to a peaceful existence finally led to a physical confrontation between Dona and Jeff. I had to forcibly pull them apart one eventful evening. That was the culmination of the antagonistic chasm that existed between the two people who were most prominent in my life. I later learned that the mutual "hate" they harbored for each other (as well as fear on Dona's part) was the direct cause for Dona viewing our relationship as untenable. Other problems developed between us as well, so we separated in 1982 for a year. Our love for each other enabled us to reunite, but our problems - especially concerning Jeff - persisted, with the whole relationship coming to a final halt in 1987. Some might say that's not a bad run for a relationship these days, but if we had found the right therapist/counselor, we should have lasted a lifetime. That's how strongly we felt about each other. The combination of circumstances and a lack of application (and acceptance) of basic "Men Are From Mars; Women Are From Venus" precepts doomed what was the ultimate in relationships, not only from our respective perspectives, but from our friends as well.

I want to illustrate two incidents as examples of how deep our emotions ran for each of us. They were very similar in context and presentation.

"The Love Of My Life," Dona with favorite beverage.

The first example, one of many, is as follows. We lived in Tustin, which is in the middle of Orange County, one of the principle bedroom communities for the commuters who, like me, worked in Los Angeles. At the time, I was the Corporate Security Director for Vidal Sassoon, Inc., our offices being in the "twin towers" of Century City adjacent to Beverly Hills, a fifty-mile one-way distance from our abode. Dona was in her natural element (I affectionately called her my "perpetual teenager") working at Disneyland as a Graphic Design Buyer, her office being a scant ten miles from home. That meant I was out the door much earlier than she. Escorting me to my car at "zero dark thirty" - an old Marine Corps expression for a very early hour in the morning - Dona would, as I drove away, shed voluminous tears of loss. I never knew this, until one morning I looked in the rear view mirror and saw her wipe away the tears. Believing something was amiss, I backed my car to the driveway. She then revealed that she uncontrollably felt a loss of my presence, even though she knew I was to return later that evening. The tears were the by-product of her emotions of love, she related to me, so deep-seated that even my momentary departure caused her to be saddened. Now there is a heart-tugger! I, too, had instantaneous tears at this revelation. It was a bonding that uniquely and graphically proved to each of us how strong our love was.

The second example, as I mentioned, was similar in nature, but indeed for me more touching and dire in its content. In October 1986, following Vidal selling his company - with all positions being eliminated by the new owner (Richardson-Vicks, which one year later sold the firm to Procter-Gamble), I began a vocational relationship with General Dynamics in San Diego. That company wanted me to be nearer their plant site, so they offered me a relocation package I couldn't refuse. Actually, I wanted Dona to stay in our Tustin home, but she couldn't bear the thought of sharing it with a roommate (it would have been virtually impossible for us to afford two house payments). It took a year for us to sell our castle (figuratively speaking, of course, but we regarded that cul-de-sac home, with its pool, large back and side yards, and enormous patio, which was the site of many parties and personal activities, as our most cherished castle).

Sadly, our castle was no longer ours. Because Dona didn't want the heavy-traffic commute between San Diego and Anaheim, and she wanted to retain her job at Disneyland, she chose to move back in with her father in El Segundo for the easier reverse-traffic drive. I was now settled in a house in San Diego. On the weekend that Dona was to vacate "our" place, we spent our last days, hours, and then minutes (it seemed like an eternity waiting for the moment to arrive when I would go out the door Monday morning for the last time). Not only was our embrace at my car tear-filled, but the drive to San Diego had me likewise full of emotion. It wasn't like we would never see each other again; it did mark the end of an era, if you will. This was "our" home - the only one we would own together - and abandoning it was no easy task. We had many fond memories at 13158 Hickory Branch Road, and we also had some negative trials and tribulations, unfortunately. Our relationship was not yet over; the thought and reality of leaving our castle was simply too much. The tears of sadness in departing from our home were really a reflection of our special - that overused but accurate word again - love that we shared.

As with other matters addressed in this capsulized book, I could write a separate and lengthy doctoral thesis on my relationship with this former "Miss El Segundo" (come to think of it, Candy - wife #2 - was a former "Miss Manhattan Beach" - I was really on a roll for attracting beauty queens!). Let me list just a few topics I could address:

☐ Why it wasn't necessary for us to get married: a piece of paper wasn't important for us - the relationship and all of its connotations were.

☐ Our trips to Hawaii and Washington, D.C., in conjunction with my duties as a "honcho" within my professional association: the good, the bad, and the ugly.

☐ The joys we shared as "parents" to my visiting daughters during their growth years: the experiences in our pool, on the beach, at Disneyland functions, etc.

☐ The year of separation: the reasons, the anguish, and the reconciliation.

☐ My intellectual approach to issues versus her "street smarts:" we never could get over that hump.

☐ Her unnecessary inferiority complex and her real anxiety syndrome: these enigmas were a disservice to her and a travesty to a "benevolent" God for this gorgeous and life-filled dynamo.

☐ Her father's influence and funeral: a man admired by his community for his volunteer work with high school athletics, a solidifying lighthouse and refuge for a sometimes confused daughter, and my contribution to Dona's sense of security upon his death, especially considering how the opposite was true when Candy's father passed on.

☐ Our tortured meetings as "friends" following our "marital" demise and her subsequent marriage: her marriage is solid, but our love - different now and diminished by reality - is still there (for me anyway).

☐ Why did it end?: June 5, 1987, our last "anniversary" is a day of infamy - as FDR said about December 7, 1941 - for me; no matter how much I've learned through the years, there are still some things I'll never understand.

Dona (It's the Spanish spelling of Donna, with its implications of royalty, even though she discovered her origins are French, including being related to the French trapper character from James Michener's book "Centennial") is totally out of my life now (her choice). I don't know about her, but I still think of "us" and how we should have corrected our problems, given the supreme love we felt for each other. Every female that I've mentioned on these pages has affected me in one way or another - that's why they're identified herein. But Dona stands by herself in my image of potential idealism. Sure, she (I should say "we") wasn't perfect and her minor imperfections greatly influenced my negative responses to her demeanor, as well as to the eventual termination of our relationship. I wish we were both smarter.

Chapter 22   Frank Bell's Suicide

I have seen death many times, but I was not prepared for May 4, 1980. With two combat tours in Viet Nam, as well as a couple of incidents I witness in flight training and the passing of my father in 1976, I thought I was somewhat hardened to the inevitability of death. However, when the grim reaper pays a visit unexpectedly, it has devastating consequences.

As mentioned elsewhere, I consider some of my best friends those people with whom I interacted with in the Marine Corps. In Chapter 8, I identified Dick Chapman and I as being two members of a sub-click within our squadron. Frank Bell was also part of that group. "Ding-Dong," a nickname he didn't care for, was a lanky and amiable San Diego native who demonstrated volleyball skills at San Diego State University. As far as I know, he never had a harsh word for anyone. Unassuming, easy-going, and yet professional to the hilt, Frank was a valuable asset to the Marine Corps and to his friends, one of whom I was fortunate enough to be.

Marines, like other military personnel, move around quite a bit. After our joint service together in HMM-163 for three years, we went our separate ways in our duty assignments, never again even being at the same military installation. He put in his twenty plus years and retired as a lieutenant colonel. He took up residence in the house he inherited from his parents, the beach front home in which he was raised in the Mission Beach section of San Diego. That is when we re-established contact. It was to become a civilian friendship - too short-lived - based on our military and aviation commonality, but one of greater depth and emotional impact.

Frank and his new bride (#2 - Pat, interestingly, given my first wife's name, whom Frank knew, of course, from HMM-163) decided on San Diego as their "retirement" residence rather than her native Denver (again interesting, since that's where my Pat now lives). Frank's Pat continues her career pursuits, but he chose the gentleman sailor's existence, spending most of his time on his boat in Mission Bay and surrounding seas. I have forgotten how we came together (I think it was at a '78 "welcome back to California" party thrown for the vacationing Chapmans by our mutual friend Linda, who was formerly married to another HMM-163 squadron mate, Jerry Nicholson), but Frank and Pat coupled very nicely with Dona and me. We spent time at his beach home, in the pool at our Tustin pad, and at various restaurants/pubs in San Diego Count. It was a close foursome.

I was scheduled to start my new job as the Corporate Security Manager for Vidal Sassoon, Inc. in Century City (Los Angeles) on May 5, 1980 - Dona's and my anniversary of our meeting on the Hughes Aircraft Company volleyball court - following my seven-year tenure of frustration at Hughes. It was an exciting time for me and I relished the challenge. The day also had great significance for me personally, given the aforementioned anniversary.

On Sunday afternoon (May 4, 1980), Dona picked up the ringing telephone at our home in Tustin. She exuberantly said "Hi" to the other party and then, with somewhat of a puzzled look of concern, handed me the receiver. Pat Bell was on the line. With surprisingly unemotional detachment, which I in retrospect wrote off to shock, she informed me that Frank had killed himself a couple of days before. My knees buckled and I almost fell down from my standing position. Dona stood by not knowing what was going on. Pat further elaborated that Frank had driven his car into the garage, closed the garage door, and sat in the vehicle until the carbon monoxide took effect. His brother found the body the next morning, Pat explained that she was visiting friends elsewhere in San Diego that night. Pat then invited us to a memorial service the next day - Monday, May 5, 1980.

The shock was probably the most devastating I have ever experienced. I had just lost my best friend, and I didn't know why such a thing could have happened. There was no reason for such a drastic act, as far as I know. I subsequently learned, however, that Frank had been deeply distraught over the death of his eighteen-year-old son, Mike. Mike was a sickly young man with all sorts of physical problems throughout his youth. His ills finally caught up with him sometime prior to Pat's call to me on May 4, 1980. Unfortunately, I didn't know about Mike's death, so I wasn't there for Frank for consoling purposes. I was just not informed.

After I called Sassoon's Director of Personnel requesting a day's delay in reporting for duty, Dona and I went to San Diego for the memorial service. It was a sad and somber drive from Tustin to Mission Beach. The service did not include a display of the casket, but I observed it in a side room, where I said my final farewells and Semper Fi to Frank. The actual services, as conducted by a rather conventional pastor, alienated me. Instead of singing Frank's praised, he requested divine forgiveness for Frank's "sin" of suicide. The program did not allow for friends or relatives to speak their minds. I almost broke the sacred silence, at the conclusion of the pastor's cold utterances, by rising and proclaiming Frank's virtues as a comrade-in-arms and friend, but I didn't, believing that the service was the way Pat wanted it. To this day I regret not speaking my piece. Frank deserved a better send-off.

Frank Bell, with post-USMC beard, checks out Michelle's new Christmas watch.

Following the so-called eulogy, I spoke with Frank's brother and learned that Frank and Pat had been ostensibly experiencing marital problems of which I knew nothing. Apparently, Frank didn't even totally confide with his brother (or other San Diego friends), let alone me. I did not broach the subject with Pat at the service, instead deferring the matter to a later date, given that she told us she'd be in touch with us following a brief visit to Denver. We never heard from Pat again.

The true reason(s) for Frank's suicide remains a mystery to me. I have great remorse over the loss, especially in the fact that Frank did not approach me with his problems. Perhaps I could have negated his abrupt action. It really bothers me that he apparently did not have confidence in me as a friend to help him through his concerns, whatever they were. But people sometimes do strange things out of character during times of depression. I know; I've been there. Depression is a deprecating state of mind. I certainly don't blame Frank for his inappropriate action; I just wish he had been more open to me - or someone - in order to preclude his final act. I miss him. He was a friend, and that carries a lot of weight for me. I have never gotten over my loss.

Chapter 23   Jim and Shirley Royer

Since I've been a civilian, I haven't made many friends very easily. Sure, many acquaintances. For me, however, there has to be a bond of commonality for someone to enter my inner circle. Usually that commonality was for the individual to have has a military background. Most of my "best" friends are still from my Marine Corps days, despite their geographic remoteness. It is also true that I formed several friendships during my bachelorhood in Hermosa Beach. That group of people were close knit and tied by the mutuality of the party scene. But their closeness was short-lived, for must of us splintered to other interests and/or geographic locations.

I'll tell you about an exception to my military commonality "rule." I briefly mentioned elsewhere that I was actively involved in a professional association - named the American Society for Industrial Security (ASIS for short) - during my corporate security management days. I assumed many voluntary leadership roles in that organization early in that career. Initially I was the Greater Los Angeles Chapter Newsletter Editor for several years. (I learned the writing, information gathering, and editing/publishing aspects.) Almost concurrently, I worked my way up the ladder of the chapter's hierarchy, finally being elected to the chapter chairman role in 1980. A year later the ASIS international president asked me to be the regional vice president for our region (CA, NV, and HI). Finally, I was elected by the entire international membership to the International Board of Directors, serving the 1983-85 term. I could also write a separate book on those activities; in fact, I started one addressing my perspectives of the activities of the board, but I got lazy, put it aside, and now it is no longer a timely issue.

Again, the theme of this book is "Affected." I want to bring to the forefront a husband and wife team within the ASIS framework who had the effect of friendship and, in Jim's case, profound admiration by me for his leadership traits.

I first met Jim Royer when we were both regional vice presidents (RVPs) for ASIS, he representing the OH/IL/IN region. He first came to my attention in January 1981 at our initial leadership meeting in Washington, D.C., he being appointed secretarial duties by the President for our RVP meeting. We did not, however, have occasion to interact socially. That was remedied at our June meeting in St. Louis. Both Jim and I arrived a bit early, so we reintroduced ourselves and adjourned to a near-by pub to get better acquainted. We hit it off immediately. There was no commonality of a military background. He was a former Cincinnati cop, so perhaps my FBI experience was the catalyst for conversation.

Although we met again at our September meeting (I have forgotten the site), we really didn't keep in touch in between. At that association's annual seminar (convention, if you like) in September, I had the opportunity to meet Jim's wife, Shirley. We too hit it off. Both Jim and Shirley were similarly warm, open, and expressive toward Dona and me. I was soon to learn that many of our associations didn't care much for Jim's projection of abruptness, callousness, biting verbiage, and hard-nose demeanor, but I found it refreshing and straight-forward, when compared to some back-stabbing, wishy-washy, and untrustworthy civilians I've met, particularly within the

ASIS national leadership scenario (my experiences on the board were considerably different from the camaraderie at the local chapter level). I thought Jim's bark was worse than his bit, and I found Shirley to be a contrasting compliment to Jim brusqueness with her graciousness and charm.

1984 Board of Directors
American Society for Industrial Security

Jim Royer and author (standing far left).

I'd like to relate one hilarious episode that I shared with the Royers. At the January 1983 national leadership meeting, I learned that Shirley's birthday fell during that week. A bunch of us in our tuxedos left the President's Reception to seek a local establishment for dinner. We were pretty much under the influence of the free libations at the reception. In a clandestine manner, I asked our waiter to bring a bottle of champagne for a birthday toast. He asked me what label; I left it up to his discretion. Without examining the bottle that he brought, we had our toast and our dinner. When the waiter handed me my check, it was for one hundred and five dollars. It thought it was for the entire dinner for all twelve of us. Making an inquiry, he informed me that it was for the one bottle of Dom Perignon, the most expensive Champagne on the wine list. Believing that I had been fleeced, I approached the maitre d' to resolve this matter. I told him that I was willing to pay the tab, but I thought our waiter had taken advantage of my ambivalence about a label. He agreed, reducing the tab by half. You had to be there in order to appreciate the hilarity of it all. The incident still serves as a stimulating piece of conversation when the Royers and I get together. To cap it off, I mailed a three-pack of Dom Perignon to them for a subsequent Christmas gift. A fitting follow-up to a humorous incident.

The friendship that I had established with Jim and Shirley was to take on greater dimensions when we were both elected to the ASIS Board of Directors (he preceded me by a year). We were both interested in change. We believed that the self-perpetuating leadership (the paid executive director was a permanent employee of the association, while the president and his staff were volunteers elected from within the entire board) had lost sight of certain issues, primarily the degree of the education programs presented by the Society. We also disagreed with certain unwritten policies (e.g., a first year board member should only be seen and not heard - what a ridiculous loss of valuable contributions during a third of a given director's term) and with the method of selection of the nominees for the officers billets (e.g., president, VP, secretary/treasurer). For years the executive director had his way running the organization. He did a fine job in expanding the Society (about four thousand members when I joined in 1973; now about twenty-five thousand world-wide with about two hundred and ten chapters in almost every industrialized country, including Moscow), but nobody ever questioned his methods or perspectives. This "good ol'" boy attitude needed change, and Jim and I (with another board member - Shirley Krieger from Phoenix) led the way to the 1984 revolution (or "Chicago Coup," as I labeled it). The annual seminar/election was held in Chicago that year.

Jim was not shy about assuming leadership reins. He did his homework on issues at hand. His persuasive powers, even with his harsh tonality, were effective and "held" regarding credibility. I don't want to get into all of the subtle and not-so-subtle conflicts and issues we addressed; let the "Chicago Coup" suffice as an illustration of Jim's magnetic leadership that not only influenced me, but 51 percent of the voting board members.

A synopsis of the 1984 "Chicago Coup" ran like this. Jim, Shirley Krieger, and I were displeased, as I mentioned above, with the officer selection process, as well as with some of the programs being approved by the self-perpetuating officers of immediately preceding years. Behind the scenes, we were able to convince the majority of the twenty-one-person body that change was needed. I was a bit concerned about the reaction of a couple of the members of the executive committee. I considered the 1984 president a quasi-friend; in fact, I hosted a "welcome aboard" party of ASIS Southern California dignitaries at my home a couple of years earlier when he relocated to Los Angeles from St. Louis for a new job. Similarly, an heir-apparent to the presidency a couple of years down the road was a guy I served with in the FBI in Seattle (he was more senior than I in the Bureau). In different ways, they were both affected by the "Chicago Coup," and I had to be eloquent and convincing in explaining my role and the reasons why to them.

Normally, it was a routine process electing the Executive Committee. Although nominations were solicited "from the floor," in accordance with Roberts Rules of Order, in the past the nominated slate (as selected by the outgoing Executive Committee) received a unanimous "rubber-stamp" affirmation. Not this time. We had it all planned out as to who would offer alternative nominations, and since we had all of our "ducks lined up," it was a "shoe-in" that our slate would be elected. When the nominations were offered, several chins dropped, especially those on the Executive Committee and the Executive Director. In accomplishing our game plan, Jim drew the most flack, including from the Council of Past Presidents (the good ol'" boy group of years past), as almost everyone believed that Jim was the organizer (he was not alone, as I said). He took most of the heat and handled it in an exemplary fashion. Finally, ears were being opened to new perspectives and the reasons for our dissatisfaction. We - the "rabble-rousers" as we were labeled - did our job well and I still commend Jim Royer (as I did in my parting speech when my term was up) with being the guiding light and chief negotiator, stimulator, and manager of change. I can't think of a better compliment.

Jim was an inspiration to me during my active ASIS days. More importantly, both Jim and Shirley became true friends. I wish, as I do with other close friends, that we lived closer geographically in order to share more time together. I further respect and honor that friendship today, for they are the only ASIS members (besides one other local couple -Ray and Patricia Johnson from Dana Point in Orange County) who have visited me during my current battle with cancer. If friendship can be measured by total commitment, then they indeed fit the bill. Thanks, guys. You are a special couple.

Chapter 24 My Video Collection

I am a movie junkie! Well, not quite. I don't have a need to see every movie made these days, especially those teenage oriented horror flicks or other such inane garbage designed for that limited audience. My taste has always leaned toward basically three genres - musicals, comedies, and action films. And not necessarily of only the modern productions. I get as much enjoyment out of watching a vintage thirties, forties, or fifties film as I do the more technically sophisticated versions that we see today.

Why is the above and below a part of this book? Simply because the movies have had a profound effect on my growth, appreciation for others' adventures, and at times pacification of my troubled state of mind. I'll get into all of that a bit later.

My father was a motion picture projectionist. He was the guy in the theater's booth who was responsible for turning on the reels of film for the viewing pleasure of the audience. He was proud of his work, and that's an important aspect of inner peace. Dad had an opportunity once to expand his horizons by going with a friend to Hollywood (from NY) in the late twenties or early thirties to become involved in the production side of the business. After some deliberation, he declined. He was not a very ambitious man, then or as time marched on. His friend - Harry Stradling, by name - went on to become a major player in the production scene as the Director of Photography (for lack of the more accurate title) on numerous films. If Dad had acted on Mr. Stradling's invitation, our lives would have obviously been quite different. Not necessarily "better," but certainly different.

As a youngster, I always viewed my father as an important person in the motion picture business. What did I know about Hollywood? He was able to get me into the theater for free! Man, that was something. For free! Saving fifteen or twenty cents (the price of a ticket when I first began my trek into make-believe in the forties) was indeed a big deal. I probably saw more feature films, "shorts" (two-three reels), and Saturday matinee serials than any number of kids combined. No wonder I was to become a walking encyclopedia of trivia for the "silver screen" (although my memory fails me a lot).

Dad never made a lot of money in the vocation of his choosing. During the depression of the 1930s, he was one of the few who never had to hawk apples or pencils on the sidewalk to "bring home the bacon." The only diversion that people had from the agonies of reality at that time was a nickel or a dime ticket into the theater. That was one of the few industries which thrived through it all. It also meant that my dad always had a job, and one which paid rather well, considering everyone else's plight. He was proud of that. It was important to him to be a provider for his family. Unfortunately, the unionization of his business didn't do well for him. Not only didn't the union keep pace with inflation, but it apparently became involved in some questionable activities, much to the dismay of my father and his associates. I don't know the extent of his involvement or influence, but even his volunteer efforts as a Business Agent for his union went for naught. They really screwed him over, to the extent of he having no pension after almost sixty years of service.

90

Getting back on track about the influence movies had on my life. As the years went by, my knowledge of extraneous trivia grew. While in high school in New York, I had considered going to college and studying the production side of Hollywood. As many things of whim do, that kind of fell to the way-side, however. Basketball became my life, and I didn't explore the theater curriculum at such schools as USC or UCLA, which of course would have been the hub of learning the business. Even my liberal arts education at Trinity College had no focus for motion picture production. The only relevance that I remember is writing a paper on "The Hollywood Myth" for a mythology class I had taken. I drew parallels to the Greek gods and other mythological characters to the icons and movers-and-shakers of Hollywood at the time. It was a pretty good paper, as I recollect.

The perpetuation of Hollywood trivia continued in my collegiate dorms. I had a couple of roommates who were also fanatics about the movies. One in particular - Bill MacDermott, a burly lineman on the school's football team - was a Marlon Brando nut who sported a few tattoos on his arms (hence, his influence on me at age nineteen to acquire a small one on my left shoulder) and could recite the entire dialogue from "The Wild One" (Mac had seen the film about one hundred and fifty times). On evenings where we weren't engaged in a local pub's diversions, a group of us would pose questions to each other concerning which actors were in which movie, no matter how large the role, and other similar trite (but not so then; it was a serious challenge!).

I found it most interesting when the game "Trivial Pursuit" was developed in the seventies, one category being "The Silver Screen." Most of the questions in that category were not much of a challenge for me. That whole "Trivial Pursuit" entertainment value was culminated one New Year's Eve in the late seventies or early eighties when a friend of Dona (see Chapter 21) deviated from the usual drinking bash in order to set up a series of tables for a revolving game of Trivial Pursuit. We didn't pair off by couples (e.g., Dona and I), but instead randomly pulled names out of a hat. As luck would have it, I was matched with the male host (a dentist), he too priding himself on his excellence in trivia. After several hours and rotations into the different categories, he and I prevailed to the winner's circle. That will show you what a liberal arts education can do for you!

I didn't acquire a VCR until I moved to San Jose in January 1987 (hence the chronological position of this chapter in the book). A fellow security management person by the name of Greg Burns introduced me to the wonders of videos and recording from the TV. My entry into that tangential world of Hollywood was my downfall. I was hooked. I became an addict. My love for this visual art form was now manifested into a collector's passion. It didn't happen overnight, however. I figured that I would collect just a few of my all-time favorite films, primarily the epics such as "Lawrence of Arabia," "Dr. Zhivago," and "The Bridge on the River Kwai." (Note: Actually, none of the epics was my first purchase. Being a Neil Diamond fan, my first purchase was his 1980 movie "The Jazz Singer," which did not draw much critical praise, but which still stands as my most cherished videotape, as it would for any Neil Diamond aficionado.) After buying a few of those epics and learning how to record HBO movies and other specials (e.g., musical extravaganzas), I decided to branch off into other types of movies that interested me.

First came the MGM musicals of the forties, fifties, and sixties, followed by certain classic comedies of that, as well as newer, vintage. And then of course I had to have the westerns and cops-and-robbers "shoot-'em-ups." My collection wouldn't be complete unless I could display a library of ALL of my favorites (oh no, I was really hooked now!). After all, those titles would define me, and we all like to project ourselves in the best and most appropriate light available. My thought pattern was, and still is (in the collector's mode), that my book shelves had to reflect my wide-range interest in the old and the new, the sweet and the tragic, the whimsical and the serious, the action and the tender, the musical and the drama. But not just any ol'' movie; it must be of such a special interest that I'd be willing to watch it over and over again. You can't say that about many movies these days.

What is my taste? Some of the epics are cited above. I have every Neil Diamond and nearly every Barbra Striesand videotape. My other musicals include the Hollywoodized show hits such as "Singing in the Rain," "Brigadoon," "Pal Joey," all of the Rogers & Hammerstein films, "Hair," and "High Society," as well as some TV "specials", such as "Miles Davis Tribute," "Frank Sinatra's 75th Anniversary Special," "The Karen Carpenter Story," And "Carly Simon at Martha's Vineyard." The comedies range from the early classics, such as "The Egg and I," "It Happened One Night," and Charlie Chaplin's "The Great Dictator," to the newer hilarities of "Mr. Roberts" and anything else with Jack Lemmon in it, "A Fish Called Wanda," "Switch," "Arthur," the two Crocodile Dundee films, "My Cousin Vinnie," and "Splash," among others. The real (and reel) classics are there also - "Gone With The Wind," "Mutiny On The Bounty," Cagney's "White Heat," and Bogart's "The Maltese Falcon" and "Casablanca." And I relish an evening's diversion into what I describe as the "shoot-'em-ups," be they John Wayne or Clint Eastwood westerns, Arnold Schwarzaneggar trips into far-out fantasylands, the Bruce Willis/Steven Seagal/Harrison Ford style of adventures, or the individual illuminations of such actors as Paul Newman, Steve McQueen, Sean Connery, Bill Holden, or Gene Hackman. Although I don't really watch them much, I have added to my collection some "sci-fi" dazzlements, such as "Frankenstein," "Dracula," the Alien trilogy with Sigourney Weaver, "The Creature From the Black Lagoon," "Close Encounters of the Third Kind," and even Christopher Reeve's "Superman" (see Chapter 1). I also have several videos of Kim Novak, who is my Hollywood "love of my life." My current collection, in all of its grandeur, now nears a total of six hundred.

I think that the reader will be able to determine from all of the chapters of this book that I am not a couch potato. My life has been full and diverse, with many enriching people having graced my travels. But I also, as stated elsewhere in addressing self-improvement, enjoy my quiet time. That type of aloneness doesn't necessarily have to be in the physical state of being alone while pondering my navel. It could, and does, also mean sucking in whatever ambiance may be to my liking at the moment. My ability to hunker down by myself with a good book or an exciting movie is not a deviation from what I perceive to be a growth wave. No one can directly experience all the wonders of the world on a first-hand basis. That's why movies have become the true "American pastime." One is able to gain an education, to fantasize about an adventure, to vicariously experience the thrill of victory and agony of defeat while being safely within the confines of his home or a theater, and to generally relish in time and distance travel to remove what could otherwise be a hum-drum existence. The motion picture, and more predominately today the videotape, has provided a tool for escapism, a path for knowledge, and a glow for euphoria that was unrealized before Thomas Edison discovered how to put a few still photos together to form a "motion" picture. I believe I have become a more complete person because of my interest in my father's chosen profession. The music has enriched my soul, the lyrics and dialogue have broadened my articulation, and the added dimensions of foreign times and places have stimulated excitement that I would have never gained had it not been for the celluloid.

As a supreme illustration of film's pacification on my being, I still silently sing the words from "Maria" or "Tonight" from that huge classic "West Side Story" whenever I find myself in a difficult situation. I don't know why those particular sounds come to my mind, but it is on an automatic button. For instance, there were many times in combat that I got through a challenge by softly sounding off to myself those tunes from my favorite Shakespearean motif. As the King of Siam said to himself from Rogers & Hammerstein's "The King and I": "It is a puzzlement!" Without the ability to visualize from a memory or a happier situation, life's puzzlement! could prove to be over-burdensome.

Thank you, Mr. Edison, for your inventive spirit. Your impact on my well-being. peace of mind, and imagination has been enormous. And thank you Greg Burns for showing me how to manipulate that mind-boggling machine called a VCR.

Chapter 25 K.C. Anderson

Writing about my last wife is not necessarily a journey into sentimentalism, although there did exist a certain degree of passion and compassion during our brief time together. My reason for including her as a person who had an effect on my life is based on her enormous influence on my personal growth into self-improvement, primarily via the methodology of "getting in touch with my feelings."

I first met K.C., who prefers using her initials rather than her given name of Karen Claude, when I returned to Southern California from Northern California in 1989. I was house-hunting; she was house-sitting. The site was a Redondo Beach townhouse that her mother owned. My needs were specific, as I had my invalid mother living with me then (the last three years of her life; my dad was already gone). I liked the townhouse's layout, so I completed a rental agreement on the spot. K.C. interpreted my immediate actions as me having an interest in her also. She was right. Uniquely, I provided as a reference a friend (Wayne Bradshaw - see Chapter 15) from Redondo Beach, who just happened to be her financial advisor from a couple of years past. That combination guaranteed that I got the townhouse, which was soon to become the first joint occupancy for K.C. and me.

When I told Wayne of my meeting with and interest in dating K.C., he couldn't believe that I would be attracted to a woman who was somewhat different in physical stature from my previous liaisons. He had, after all, seen my preference for women from my bachelor days in Hermosa Beach (in fact, it was he who "fixed me up" with Candy, my eventual second wife). What he didn't know, however, was that K.C. had lost a considerable amount of weight since he last saw her. K.C. was not as slender as others with whom I have been seriously involved, but she was certainly within my strict parameters for dating. Besides, she had (still has) gorgeous and exotic facial features. And, as I was pleasantly pleased to learn, she was probably the best kisser I have ever known, which definitely ranks high on my list of preferences.

Not too long after K.C. and I began seeing each other, I learned that she, like Arlene (see Chapter 14) but with a different focus, was fully into "being in touch with one's feelings." I remember one early conversation. She stated that she preferred a man who is "vulnerable." At that time, my interpretation of that term was drastically different from hers. My definition had negative connotations, with an inference of weakness. Which of course was anathema to a hard-nose Marine! Little did I realize that her perspective of "vulnerability" referred to a man recognizing his inner self, his feelings about matters of importance, and his ability to communicate those matters to anyone, particularly to his mate. Well, that "feelings" stuff was foreign to me. The essence of my being, as explored by Arlene and me, took a different path toward utopia.

I initially resisted K.C.'s perspectives. I knew, however, that if I was going to pursue this relationship, I had better find out what she was talking about. After many conversations, subsequent therapy and readings, attendance at a multi-session "Life-Spring" seminar, and an "engagement encounter" with K.C., I finally awoke. I'm not here to expound the wonders and enlightening comprehension of "vulnerability" and "feeling;" I'm here to simply relate how K.C.

had and effect on me. And that she did.

My early ventures into self-improvement, self-realization, and self-actualization began, I suppose, with Arlene. It was honed to some degree during my early therapy sessions in Hermosa Beach. I took a sabbatical from my learning curve until I met K.C. In retrospect, I am amazed that my continuing growth in these matters went on a hiatus for about sixteen years. As I said in Chapter 15, the lack of such pursuits certainly contributed to the demise of my relationship with Dona.

Famous old expression: "If I knew then what I know now!"

I guess it takes someone with a real propensity for learning - no matter what the subject - to be receptive to the influence of others. It happened for me with Arlene and finally K.C., but not in between with Candy and Dona. We are all attracted to different people for different reasons. We also "fall in love" for different reasons. Most people go a lifetime without learning about themselves, interpersonal and marital relationships, and how to pursue "nirvana." There is a true Hindu definition for nirvana, but I'm using the expression to infer a self-actualization mode of finding peace and comfort in, I suppose, an air of contentment based on knowledge of spiritual and earthly matters.

Ed and K.C.'s wedding (September 21, 1990) with author's children - Michelle, Jeff, and Misty, (left-to-right)

WOW! What a sentence that was. Sorry for the pedantic presentation. I'm certainly not the man on the mountain top. And I don't profess to know it all. I have made strides, however, by being open to other perspectives. I highly recommend the exploration to everyone. You don't need a "guru;" start at your local library or book store. You just have to sincerely want to do it. Remember, everyone can change his/her behavior; you just have to want to do it.

I finally, at least in my estimation, caught up to K.C. regarding being in touch with my feelings. At least we were on the same "wave-length." My strides impressed her enough to do the marriage bit, after having lived together for a while. I think we were both hesitant though. Her passion and sex drive exceeded mine, for whatever reason. She was a compulsive personality, which bothered me. On the night before our divorce was final, when we were baring our souls, I told her that her weight bothered me. But the more I think about it, that was not one hundred percent true. We were just looking for "reasons why," and I think I was grabbing for straws, as the expressions goes.

Early in our relationship we discussed the "role reversal" aspect of our bonding, given that she had a much greater income as a "headhunter" than I did in corporate security management. I thought we had that squared away, but we evidently had varying definitions of that term. That dichotomy bit us. And we were different in several other ways as well (e.g., I am a "visual," she an "audible."). I mention all of these problem areas that led to our divorce because they superseded our (actually mine, not hers) commitment to the relationship. It happens.

She was good for me in moving me forward in my appreciation for self-improvement and awareness. She readily admits that I was good for her also, primarily in bringing her out of shell of social limitations. We had some good times together (e.g., trip to New York City and New England on our honeymoon; an exquisite Caribbean cruise with a group of her business associates) and we even enjoyed our quiet times, collectively and individually. Everyone we knew thought we were a good couple, complimenting each other well. I thought it could have been a lasting relationship, given my (and I thought her) commitment to it, our learning from each other, and our mutual willingness to pursue help when we needed it. In a retrospective analysis of my life and loves, if I had made the commitment effort of "working" on the relationship with my earlier mates as I had with K.C., I might have had a more secure and lasting marriage with any of those earlier women.

In brief, K.C.'s effect on me will be a sustaining one for the rest of my life. Whereas Pat was a dutiful Marine Corps wife, Candy was my fantasy, and Dona was my best friend and "love of my life," - I'm only referring to my "ex-wives" for purposes of this sentence - K.C. was my most comprehensive instrument for change. I wish that change had occurred earlier in my life, but since it happened when it did, K.C. draws my raves for her insights, persistence, and inspiration for my finally learning "What's it all about, Alfie?" My gratitude goes to her for her wisdom, her passion (the sexual side of our relationship was indeed different and expanding for me), and her semi-tolerance in assisting me through my last career change from the security world to outplacement services (e.g., writing of resumes and teaching of interviewing and networking techniques).

Chapter 26 Nancy Glenning

I conclude my list of influential people in my life with this rare and extraordinary "Florence Nightingale." Because of my present medical situation, I suspect that Nancy will be the last woman in my life, regardless of my life span. Why? Because I have made a commitment to her, given her dedication to caring for me during my illness, which may or may not be terminal (the jury is still out).

I have known Nancy since late 1984. When I joined the General Dynamics security staff, she was one of the administrative people who reported to me. I took an instant liking to her (platonic only, as I knew intra-office affairs could prove dangerous) for her sarcastic humor, which paralleled mine. I called her "Ms. Rickles" in deference to the comedian Don Rickles. However, we did date for a while after I left General Dynamics, although I think she knew I was still hurting and in love with Dona following that relationship termination.

Following my divorce from K.C., we dated again briefly. In August of 1994, I moved in with my ol' Marine Corps drinking buddy, Christine Sherry, in Escondido. My daughter Misty had just graduated from high school in Tustin (in Orange County) and had "gone off on her own." I had a desire to buy a house in San Diego County, so Christine invited me to use her hill-top hacienda as a home base during my house-hunting.

After going through another short-lived romance with a spunky lady half my size in San Diego, but before I was diagnosed with cancer, Nancy and I again dated briefly. In mid-February 1995, after going through about eight months of increasingly not being able to swallow, I went to Scripps Clinic in La Jolla. None of my doctors/specialists in Orange County could properly diagnose my problem, a situation which later precipitated me initiating (and winning) a medical malpractice lawsuit against them. When the people at Scripps stated I had an advanced malignant tumor at the base of my tongue, radiation treatment was the therapy of choice. It was to be a debilitating process, including the recovery period, with a prognosis that was not very encouraging (only about ten percent of people with my type of cancer survive).

Author at 1995 housewarming party with two co-wives (Candy and K.C.) and care-giver and supreme friend, Nancy Glenning.

Although I could have stayed at Christine's place (I had made an offer on a townhouse in Escondido by then, but had to withdraw it due to the medical prognosis), Nancy stepped forward and volunteered to take care of me at her place in San Diego, no matter what the outcome. I warned her of the possibilities, but she was adamant. Obviously, the lady cared for me, later admitting that she had been in love with me since our first dating episodes.

So I moved in with Nancy. She was a real God-send. Although Christine has been a good friend for many years, I'm not sure she would have been receptive to being my "care-giver." It's a tough job. In brief, Nancy did whatever was necessary to make me comfortable. Throughout this ordeal, I had lost about fifty-sixty pounds. My strength ebbed. But.....my PMA (Positive Mental Attitude) prevailed. After a $6\frac{1}{2}$ week radiation program of two intense dosages per day, the tumor disappeared. Obviously, we all were elated. And then I threw the "monkey wrench" into Nancy's plans. I suspect that she wanted me to stay with her forever. After receiving the good news from my doctor, however, I told her I wanted to re-initiate my search for my own place. After that scare, I essentially needed my own space.

For the next 6 months, I reveled in being surrounded again by my own possessions/furniture in another townhouse that I purchased in Escondido. I was gaining weight and was generally feeling pretty good in my recovery. I also maintained liaison with Nancy in a very casual but friendship manner. I really didn't want any ties or relationships at that time; in fact, I didn't date or pursue anyone (I probably couldn't have anyway, given my weakened state).

Disaster struck in December 1995. I was having tremendous headaches, losing weight, and feeling lousy. In early January 1996, my doctor hospitalized me. I was one hundred and thirty-one pounds (my normal weight for years was a solid two hundred and five). There was no evidence (e.g., MRI) that the cancer had returned, but one of my doctors labeled me as "terminal."

Well, I fooled them again. After a week of stabilizing my body in the hospital, I was released to recover at home. But what home? Nancy again stepped forward, volunteering to nurse me back to health (hopefully). I was in worse shape this time around. They even had hospice service made available to me, that of course being for terminally ill people only.

Once again, my PMA kicked in. I got better. To such an extent that the hospice services were removed. Unfortunately, a couple of months later a biopsy revealed that the tumor on my tongue had returned, big time. Nancy and I discussed the options with several doctors, finally deciding on chemotherapy instead of surgery, the latter having a greater chance for complications than cure. At this writing, I am about to have my third dosage on a game plan of a chemo session every three weeks. An MRI after the second application revealed a slight shrinkage of the tumor, so we're all optimistic. My new oncologist says his success rate with patients with similar problems is seventy percent plus. Maybe I'll get lucky again.

To summarize Nancy's contribution to my recovery and her overall effect on my life and well-being, I have to reach to the very essence of my soul to find the love and appreciation I have

98

for her. The large dosages of morphine (a pain controller) to which I've been subjected has dulled my sex drive. Consequently, ours is not a physical relationship. It just ain't there! Probably not even if Kim Novak were at hand (she's been my Hollywood fantasy for years and years). Nevertheless, Nancy has always been there for me, with no demands or questions asked. Her love must be boundless, her strength and resolve must be unlimited, and her devotion must be unparalleled in all of mankind. Perhaps the latter is a bit of an exaggeration, but she has been a very rare jewel for me.

Immediately before and even after I had my relapse, Candy (she had returned to Southern California at the same time as Misty, she living in Manhattan Beach) and I had discussed the possibility of us reuniting. She is not the same flighty person I knew and married when she was twenty-two. The vision of "Love is lovelier the second time around" crossed my mind and heart. Candy was, after all, the mother of Misty, my "love child" if you will, my only natural-born offspring, and a true blessing to me since she came to live with me at age sixteen in 1993.

The fantasy of Candy and me becoming a couple again never came to fruition. I recognized how much Nancy had done for me. I simply could not disillusion her again by departing her home as soon as I was feeling halfway decent. So I made a commitment to Nancy that I was hers as long as she wanted me around. I owe her that much. Her happiness is important to me. She has given so much to me that she deserves whatever happiness I can provide, no matter what my medical status or longevity might be. I have learned that love is different with different people. Our relationship is different from others I've had, especially since I cannot provide physical pleasures, at least for now. But if I can give to her as she has given to me, then I think the calling of my last years (or months, if the chemo doesn't work) has to be to Nancy. Her effect on me transcends all other possibilities. Not only because she deserves it, but because giving is truly better than receiving.

I believe another postscript is warranted here. A review of this chapter, not only by the title holder of this chapter but by others as well, has led to certain misperceptions and a variance from the intent of this writing. Recognizing that subjectivity can be present if the words are not explicitly clear, I would like to emphasize the importance of Nancy in my life and the true focus of my commitment to her, per my original intent.

All relationships are different. That is an absolute fact! My commitment - and that is a strong word, at least in my vocabulary - to any relationship varies, depending on the circumstances, euphoria, and/or projection of a future to that particular individual. My commitment to Nancy is probably the strongest of any relationship I've had, in the sense of maturity and recognition of reality. I may have had a stronger emotional tie (e.g., to Dona, as the "love of my life") because of circumstances, but it is superseded in a sense by my dedication to Nancy, regardless of the prognosis or outcome of my present medical situation. I believe that this type of love transcends the elements of momentary (however long it may be) attraction and infatuation. They (whoever "they" are) say that true, lasting, and sincere love is based first on friendship and then augmented by the physical and euphoric traits so readily identified with a passion based on momentary (and usually transitory) infatuation. Until now, all of my previous relationships had that connotation of a physical attraction first, followed by a relative degree of "friendship." Look at my track record. I have indeed been a vagabond in my relationships, primarily because they were not based on friendship, first and foremost.

In the past, I have always believed that in order to consummate a relationship, it was necessary to have been physically attracted to a woman. I have read extensively that the opposite is true. But I have not fully accepted it as reality until Nancy came into my life. True, we initially "dated," but that was short lived. Friendships evolve because of various circumstances. And not every friendship with a member of the opposite results in a marital (or permanent, without the need for a state-sanctioned document) commitment. But when a commitment results from a friendship, that can seal a true, permanent, and most gratifying relationship. That is what has occurred with Nancy. There have been several developments in our continuum that have led to my feeling of commitment. For instance, the "Ms. Rickles" commonality, the ability to communicate on a plane of reality without fear of "upsetting" the friend, and her commitment to me, not only during my illness, but her long-standing appreciation for me as a person, with all of my foibles.

In totality, it takes that kind of friendship to make a real relationship last. It has taken me a long time to figure that out. Perhaps my intellectual recognition has finally melted into sync with my emotional acceptance of "What's it all about, Alfie?" I can now say that my life is full. It's just unfortunate that it took a major illness to bring it to light for me. But it's never too late, no matter how much time I have left. I am content.

Author's Biography

Edward J. Anderson has a diverse background, with professional experience in both the public and private sectors. He originally hails from Mt. Kisco, NY, where his accomplishments as a high school athlete led to a collegiate basketball scholarship. Upon graduating from Trinity College in Hartford, CT, with a Bachelor of Arts degree in History and Government, he entered the Marine Corps' Officer Candidate School. Successfully achieving a commission as a Second Lieutenant, he thereafter completed the Naval Flight School at Pensacola, FL. As a Naval Aviator, he served eleven years as a Marine Corps helicopter pilot, including two tours in Viet Nam.

Author before 50-pound weight loss from recent illness.

In making a major career change into law enforcement, Ed was designated a Special Agent with the FBI in 1971. After two years of service with that organization, he transferred that training to the private sector by becoming a corporate security management practitioner. For the next seventeen years, he served in such capacities as Security Investigator, Manager of Loss Prevention, and Director of Corporate Security for Hughes Aircraft Company, Vidal Sassoon, Inc., General Dynamics, FMC, Pic 'N' Save, and The Upper Deck Company.

Another career change took Ed into the outplacement services field, where he specialized in writing resumes and teaching networking, interviewing, and negotiation techniques for clients of major firms in that business. Prior to his recent major illness, which precipitated his premature retirement, he operated his own firm in that arena.

Ed has earned a Master's degree in Public Administration, with concentrations in Criminal Justice Administration and Organizational Theory/Behavior/Development. He has been active in a professional association, serving as its Greater Los Angeles Chapter Chairman, Regional Vice President, and as a member of its international Board of Directors. He also has planned, organized, and conducted several major seminars. As a writer, Ed has had several articles published in local and national periodicals, primarily pertaining to the development of comprehensive security programs.

"Affected" is his first completed book, but he began another ten years ago relating to his experience as a volunteer in his professional association. It is in the process of being completed.

Order Form

[] Company
Contact:
Bus Number: (   )
Fax Number: (   )

[] Individual

Your Name:
Address
City
State   Zip

Sales Tax:
Please add 7.75% for books shipped within California

Prices:
Price of book: $13.95 per book for paperback edition

# of books ordered [   ]

Shipping:
$ 3.00 shipping/handling first book and $ 1.00 for each
additional book on same order
Air Mail: $ 4.00 per book

Payment:
(   ) check   (   ) money order
(   ) cashier's check

Make check/money order/cashier's check payable to:
Gwendolyn Evans

Mail payment to: **Pinnacle-Syatt Publications**
                        535 Calle Capistrano
                        San Marcos, CA 92069-8306

Allow 2 to 5 business days for delivery. Thank you in advance for your order!

Order Form

[] Company
Contact:
Bus Number: (   )
Fax Number: (   )

[] Individual

Your Name:
Address
City
State   Zip

Sales Tax:
Please add 7.75% for books shipped within California

Prices:
Price of book: $13.95 per book for paperback edition

# of books ordered [   ]

Shipping:
$ 3.00 shipping/handling first book and $ 1.00 for each
additional book on same order
Air Mail: $ 4.00 per book

Payment:
(   ) check   (   ) money order
(   ) cashier's check

Make check/money order/cashier's check payable to:
Gwendolyn Evans

Mail payment to: **Pinnacle-Syatt Publications**
                        535 Calle Capistrano
                        San Marcos, CA 92069-8306

Allow 2 to 5 business days for delivery. Thank you in advance for your order!

Order Form

[] Company
Contact:
Bus Number: (   )
Fax Number: (   )

[] Individual

Your Name:
Address
City
State   Zip

Sales Tax:
Please add 7.75% for books shipped within California

Prices:
Price of book: $13.95 per book for paperback edition

# of books ordered [   ]

Shipping:
$ 3.00 shipping/handling first book and $ 1.00 for each additional book on same order
Air Mail: $ 4.00 per book

Payment:
(   ) check   (   ) money order
(   ) cashier's check

Make check/money order/cashier's check payable to:
Gwendolyn Evans

Mail payment to: **Pinnacle-Syatt Publications**
535 Calle Capistrano
San Marcos, CA 92069-8306

Allow 2 to 5 business days for delivery. Thank you in advance for your order!